Preaching Matters

Effective Preaching for Changing Times

Dr. Aaron L. Chapman

authorHOUSE®

AuthorHouse™
1663 Liberty Drive
Bloomington, IN 47403
www.authorhouse.com
Phone: 1 (800) 839-8640

Published by AuthorHouse 06/11/2020

ISBN: 978-1-7283-6392-9 (sc)
ISBN: 978-1-7283-6391-2 (e)

Contents

Dedication

As I reflect at the completion of this project, I can't help but thank God for my wife Valarie and my two children Aaron and Destiny. I am forever grateful for your constant support, love and understanding.

I would like to also express my sincere appreciation for my mother, Faye Chapman. Mom, you are a phenomenal woman of God. You continue to motivate me with your tireless strength, unyielding support and your loving demands for me to strive for personal growth as well as aiding in the growth of my fellow man.

To Mr Baskin, I am honored to have you in my life. Thank you for reviewing this manuscript and making sure that this project was presented with excellence.

In loving memory of Pastor Ivan Hassel. This project is also dedicated in memory of you, a gentle giant! You gave me the drive to finish strong!

In loving memory of Karlton Wise. Your legacy will never die!

To all Preachers across America. I dedicate this
to you! Your preaching certainly matters!

#GOBEGREAT#Scotty

Dr. Chapman has an extreme passion for the preaching of the
gospel of Jesus Christ. He has been fully equipped for the cause of
helping the preacher of the gospel to effectively present the gospel.

Dr. F. Bernard Mitchell
Zion Hill Baptist Church
Mendenhall, MS

Introduction

What comes to mind when you hear the word Preaching? Does it move anything within you? Does this one word initiate an inner stirring, a pricking of the personal conscious or a sense of essential proclamation that leads to liberation? Preaching for countless centuries has ignited a burning sensation, reflective of the experience which crept in the lives of a couple of wandering withdrawn disciples of Christ. These followers were oblivious to the true hermeneutic of the emptiness of the tomb that supposedly and or tragically tethered their master to death forever. These nihilistic men were defaulters to the dusty roads pointing toward the destination of Emmaus in Luke 24:13-35 NASB. They cringingly articulated to an uninformed stranger their thoughts "we had hoped that he was the one". This exclamation came forth prior to the post-preaching experience. After the stranger delineated the kerygma they emphatically professed, "Were not our hearts burning within us while he was ("Christ *the stranger*") talking to us along the way." It is quite possible others are acquainted today with this burning sensation reflective of these disciples. Unfortunately, their experience is certainly contrary, a sort of alternative burning of resentment, recalling their adolescent years wrestling with the repetitive imperatives by guardians to sit up straight and heed to the preached message. A message that was expected to bring about the fulfillment of a distinct deliverance for their youthful souls.

Preaching? Preaching? Expressed intentionally with a doubled interrogative as a major concern. Does this term matter? As a matter of fact, what is Preaching? We can easily call for Siri and Alexa to assist in answering that question or just go to the gods of google according to Brianna Parker. These sources often provide us with a shallow secular understanding of the term, totally detached from the sacred synopsis of its divine purpose. The interrogative screams to be answered, why does preaching matter if we do not even agree on its ontology? What is preaching? There is a stirring statement concerning the purposeful genesis of preaching printed in the text *Contemporary Preaching*. Let us take note of the writers understanding concerning the function and fruit of preaching:

"Thus, preaching springs from the truth that God has spoken in word and deed and that He has chosen human vessels to bear witness to Himself and His gospel. We speak because we can not be silent — we speak because GOD HAS SPOKEN!"
(Duduit 1992, 14)

While we are discussing the fabulous facets of preaching, we must also consider circles where preaching lacks notoriety. Contrary to the populace of ecclesiastical preunderstanding, there is a skeptical non-religious climate where there are individuals who are not immediately familiar with the local church verbiage, Preaching. Frankly I concur, it is not a far stretch to claim that there are individuals that have never come across the term preaching and or who have never experienced the true essence of it. These homiletical deprived individuals may currently possess a gross deficient of insight and interaction with these terms preach, preacher, and preaching but this does not have to be their conclusive experience.

The local church enjoyed homiletic home court advantage. Hearers who visited these hallow grounds had roots or exposure to the vernacular of the church, but recently the rug of working knowledge of preaching norms have been totally pulled from underneath the church. Maybe it is time to revisit the necessity of a radical reacquaintance of the term preaching; while giving rise to an introspective introduction of its intricacies for those hibernating in ecclesiastical isolation.

The utilitarian nature of preaching has been explored by several homileticians and heralds throughout history, who have their fingerprints embroidered across this subject matter for sure. These scholars and experienced practitioners have attempted to place preaching in a timeless capsule in an effort to keep it eschatologically fresh. Preaching has not lost its vibrancy since the origins of its birthing canal proceeding from the very mind of God. Preaching's illustrious image, and sacred silhouette is irrevocably cemented in the activity of scripture. Fred Craddock expounded on one occasion

"Is there anything else that can really be stated on the subject of preaching? Has the depths of its theological wells run dry?"

Even if it is only a tablespoon of thought lying dormant in the prescriptive bottle of this sovereignly sponsored sacred art of preaching, we owe it to the past, present and future generations; to wait with pedagogical homiletic spoons hoovering; awaiting the residue of such genius to be shared. As we continue to ponder the gravity of the essence of preaching; those who are classified as clergy can attest to the internal pathos(emotion) drawn from the warm wells of sermons bathed in their graceful stroll down memory lane! Reflect with me for a moment; when you think of preaching is it an assignment that has arrested your effort to passionately expose others to the living Christ. Preaching is a princely communicative privilege that has the power to augment humane decisions so that the "listener" can detour toward divine discoveries.

Let us pause and ponder another question that is extremely vital. Why Preaching? Communicative digital highways are bursting across the globe. In this contemporized juggernaut of post-modernity, the communicative gap is narrowing. How the church sees the world and how the world sees the church is drastically shifting. Through the technological outlets of social media platforms, networking apps, live streaming, Smart TV, Mevo, Zoom, Email, Texting etc., all of these are means of instant communication. Bryan Chapell in his text *Christ Centered Preaching* explains that:

"The impact of technology and mass communication has... made preachers question traditional approaches to preparing sermons. (He) remains convinced that an expository approach is the most fruitful as the mainstay of a pulpit ministry." (Chapell 2005, 15)

Are the best days of preaching behind it or ahead of it? Is preaching on its last good homiletic leg and there are only weak whispers beckoning an encore. Charles Spurgeon warned "You might as well expect to raise the dead by whispering in their ears, as hope to save souls by preaching to them, if it were not for the agency of the Holy Spirit. Preaching is alive and well as long as it is imbued by the power of the Holy Spirit." (Duduit 1992, 18)

In these days of Conference Calls, Facebook Live and Podcast, what significance does preaching purport? Have the origins of the Herald speaking in the courts of the community become speedily obsolete? Is preaching in need of a ministerial makeover? Considering the rapid shifts in preaching, is it still ideal for him or her to lug around a Bible and a manuscript (be it visible or invisible) delineating the gospel's options through firm exegesis among an awaiting audience. Is this rhetorical format ineffective or are Users symptomatically delusional who strain to keep alive an art form that dare I say, has died or is in rhetorical ICU! Is there a dire need for props in the pulpit and promotional tools or gimmicks to keep the congregant's attention? (Stick a pin or thumbnail here! We will return to this discussion in a later chapter). Is this communicative style of heralding the gospel from the pulpit without the spiritual garnish still appropriate and a kingdom best practice for progressing the gospel in a millennial era?

There has even been an inquiry raised by Brianna Parker in her book entitled *"What Google Can't Give."* Seriously, who would have ever thought computer data and clergy declaration would become competitors oppose to being complimentary in nature? This is definitely a different view of church culture and communicative culture.

The hoovering inquiry concerning the complimentary nature or the co-existing of the online church and the effectiveness of physical oratorical communication is essential. I had no idea how illumining a recent pandemic would be in answering this theoretical question. The pandemic arrangement affirmed that tech and teaching in the church is feasible and effective! These two communicative juggernauts co-existed with integrity as a temporary solution. This became evident immediately after the Governor of Michigan executed an Executive Order enforcing social distancing (which was also authorized by the governing bodies) of being at least 6 feet from another human being. This was necessary in the attempt to flatten the curve of the Covid-19 virus. The reduction of the number of people allowed to socially gather dropped to as low as ten people based on safety precautions. This executive order forced the churches in March 2020 to deal with the realities of online worship with empty churches.

The church was forced to consider this option which prior to this it was unimaginable. Those church leaders who predicted the trend believed it was at least another decade away from implementation. But, churches had to recalibrate or adjust to deal with the here and now! Being an eyewitness to this adjustment, it became clear that those who were not substantive in their preaching approach struggled, because they could not use crowd interaction as a crutch. Stephen Rummage furnished some effective strategies of preaching with no one immediately present, in an effort to relieve the sermonic sting. This was not the only era of preaching that was forced to face the challenges presented between technology and preaching.

Forty years earlier in the mid 1980's we uncovered in the written text *Preacher and Preaching,* which bears a compilation of homiletic essays concerning preaching. J.I. Packer in the opening essay tackled the subject matter "why preaching?" Let's consider his profound response to this question:

> "To be an honest question, expressing honest uncertainty as to whether there is a viable rationale for pulpit work in our time. I blame no one for raising the question- indeed, I see many reasons why thoughtful people might well raise it.... Whose question is it though? Does it come from a discouraged preacher? Or from a weary listener? Or from a pastoral organizer who wants more time for other things and grudges hours earmarked for sermon preparation? Or from a student communication theory, who doubts whether pulpit

monologue can ever convey as much as dialogue or discussion, or an audio-visual film presentation or TV?" (Packer 1986, 1)

There is certainly nothing wrong with the query of the quest for effective preaching in this present day as it was examined in the mid 1980's but the course of action to accomplish the communicative goal can become a major concern; when preaching becomes incoherent to the listener because of needless extras that accessorizes preaching, but accomplishes substandard effectiveness for the pulpit work there is a need for reevaluation.

It might be advantageous for us to ask how is it that there are preachers in ministry contemporarily that don't have ecclesiastical extravagant bells and whistles, so to speak? They stand with only the Bible, a God Sense (doctrine, theology, exegesis….), a voice and their integrity of soul. Phillip Brooks propose it's preaching through personality. I believe that this marvelous medium of mounting the pulpit with an exclusive message from God for men and women's maladies is still relevant and essential for the transformative measures needed in faith. The preacher's assignment has not been assassinated by a partisan premature retirement prior to the Parousia of Christ (Return of Christ). Rather as the conditions are becoming more and more hostile across the globe the currency of Christ centered and God exalting communication of the clergy is ever increasing and necessary.

This notion of preaching matters gripped me in a worship

experience. Pastor Terrance Gowdy was proclaiming the word of God with precision and power and he then spoke about the importance, the vitality, the power, and the influence of preaching at which time he took a pregnant pause and he stated... "Preaching Matters!". From this experience it launched me back on the creative canvas to craft a preaching text that wrestles with the relevancy of preaching, the bare bones of preaching; the nuts and bolts; the necessity of preaching; and the indispensable nature of preaching. Hopefully this leads to a reevaluation of the relevance of preaching in the local church and academia. Ridding ourselves of the attitudinal reflections that preaching is the stepchild to other theological disciplines or just an addendum to sooth the conscious of casual attenders of worship who need theological meaningless sermos (speech) each Sunday. Hopefully after turning these pages of this text it reopens the window of preaching as witness; to reconsider, reevaluate and reexamine the ontology of preaching to carefully ponder the purpose of preaching. I believe this will cause another step toward the resolution that preaching does indeed matter!

Chapter 1

Who does Preaching Matter To?

In the comedy relief film Hitch, actor Will Smith plays the character Alex "Hitch" Hitchens is an affluent matchmaker who makes his living by creating sociological situations for gentlemen to be noticed by ladies. These men lacked the autonomy to make love connections on their own. Eventually, a journalist who was obsessively determined to defame and dismantle Hitch's business captured the deadly scoop. As one of Hitch's clients Albert Brennaman was expressing the depth of his broken heart and his interest in healing his romantic relationship; Hitch demonstratively stated I'm done! It's over we adjust we move on; and we evolve so that you never have to feel like this again. There was one line that shocked me and that was Albert fired back to Hitch's dismay "Oh I get it! So you sell the stuff but you don't really believe it."

This line in this movie by Albert Brennaman to Hitch speaks volumes to the concern of divine communication known as Preaching. There is a lot of proclamation or selling of rhetoric so to speak, but do we really believe what we are proclaiming? Does preaching really matter to

1

you? Does preaching really matter to the Preacher? If Preaching doesn't matter much to those who are engaging in the spiritual practice, then it will not matter much to those who are recipients of their preaching. There is a mentality that is mended to this message by Albert and pinned to the practical for our perspective of preaching. This challenges clergy to face an introspective question. Therefore, I ask again, does Preaching Matter? The Disposition and deportment behind the question is not too far removed from the declaration of the Hebraic proverb in Homiletic terms "As a preacher (man or woman) thinketh so is he or she." Thomas Liske, after scanning for the sensibility and sacredness of the practice of preaching wrote in his text *Effective Preaching*, "Preaching has failed because somewhere preachers have failed." (Liske 1960, 15)

Preaching is serious business. Life and death is derived from the birth canal of preaching. Spurgeon admonishes that a theological analysis reveals preaching to be a deadly business. Spurgeon elaborates life, death, hell and worlds unknown may hang on the preaching and hearing of a sermon (Duduit 1992, 18) Emerson thought so much of the seriousness of effective preaching that he recorded in a journal "The ineffectiveness of preaching, speak things or hold thy peace!" If we acknowledge it or not preaching has demands; preaching bears weighty words and when we use its content, there must be a concerted effort to communicate with accuracy and openness to what God is doing during the sermon event in the local assembly.

As chosen ministers there must be a consideration of what it means to be a serious preacher. Seriousness is not a synonym for the appearance of a grimacing demeanor or visibly appearing mean. Rather to be serious is to partner intensity with intentionality. The intensity of the preacher is the passion for the purpose of God that spills over into the sermonic moment. Craddock explains that Passion *in Preaching* makes one persuasive. (Craddock 1985, 23) Preaching must reflect a discipline life that is birthed in the intimacy of study through prayer and preparation which has never been a surrogate activity of preaching excellence. John Maxwell stated in his book "The 15 Invaluable Laws of Growth" that there is a difference between being passionate and just being interested. When you are interested alone there is no immediate action that follows. The latter term intentionality suggest that the preacher places their hands on everything that they can control. This is maximization of time, space, and resources that God has availed to the preacher so that they have done everything humanly possible and that all that is left is heavenly participation. Please understand that there is nothing that can replace or substitute what God does in the life of the preacher and his/her preaching. There is a certain zone that I believe the preacher needs to find that flows naturally with his or her personality that profits not only him/her but the people of God.

Unfortunately, the words of Les Brown concerning a person's lack of passion for discipline and/or success, points an accusatory arrow toward those claiming hunger in the assignment of preaching. Les' critique was people are seriously not serious. There are preachers that are seriously not serious. James Stewart expressed "Surely there are few figures so pitiable as the disillusion minister of the Gospel."(Stewart 1946, 20) It

3

takes more than a clergy collar; it takes more than a robe; a designer suit, dress and pumps to make a great preacher. You can grasp the preaching start up kit of Doctor language; crave a title struck disposition; place a cross around your neck and lease three touch your neighbors but Preaching has a vast value that covers more than those visible trappings. How serious are you about preaching and is this truly your purpose? Are you serious about the public perception? Are you serious about the product that follows your efforts in ministry? There is a residual effect in the community, as well as in the internal cleric communing circles of the communicative science and sacred art of preaching. Barbara Brown Taylor in The Preaching Life reminds us that:

The reason why we have to address the seriousness of preaching is because the climate of ministry has become virally lax. The infection of religious irresponsibility and recklessness has infiltrated instruments of the resounding good news. This has ultimately yielded headlines of hellish and hemorrhaging heartbreak. The odds are stacked extremely high; there is a lot on the line; there is a colossal collapse that is pending for those who register for the cesspool of sin opposed to clinging to a celestial character. (Brown-Taylor 1993, 81)

Seriousness in study

If preaching truly matters, there is a need to spend a sufficient amount of time in the presence of God through meditation; reflection and petitions (prayers) made to Him. Jonathan Edwards known to some as one of the most significant theologians in American history spent as many as 13 hours a day in study for his preaching and teaching. The preparation time of the preacher needs to be a time of consecration between the preacher and Providence. There must be an uncompromising unplugging from our devices; alert tones; instant messages; incoming calls and outgoing text and all other sorts of distractions that interrupt the channel of our making an internal connection with the Eternal God. Bill Hybels in his book *Simplify* speaks of the "uncluttering of your soul". As Hybels explains this concept, he uses the example of Martha doing many things in Luke 10:38-42. Jesus redirected her after offering the diagnosis of her dilemma by saying she was distracted. The word distracted means to be pulled in all directions at once, it also conveys withdrawing oneself from one reality and being absorbed by one or two more realities simultaneously (Hybels 2014, 3). If we will engage in effective study, we must not only be in the space we must become surgical in our activity in that place. Remaining very detailed and alert in the process and listening for the gentile guiding voice of God that grooms understanding. There is a trilateral methodology of study and reflection that I advocate for the preacher who is serious about wrestling with the text. As Bob stated "When we come to the text it invites us to come and wrestle." We wrestle by

Studying the Word of God Personally

2 Timothy 2:15 in the KJV Paul encourages Timothy to "Study to show yourself approved before God." In the NASB it translates the word study as "Be diligent." The Greek Etymology translates it as "Do

your best". Paul communicates this to Timothy as an imperative, which is a command. When clergy are enlisted to engage in the work of the preaching ministry, it should never be uttered that we did not exemplify maximum effort for the progression of the people and ultimately the glory of God. Now there will be times that we are not at our best but there should never be a time that we are not endeavoring to offer our best!

Studying must become the irrevocable oxygen to the brain of our preaching. Embracing the seriousness and importance of studying places us in an holy homiletic hibernating state so that when called upon to deliver sermonic out-puts to the people of God, those waken moments of fervent exegetical in-puts made in the still moments of meditation will produce proficiency and power in the preachers proclamation.

Quiet time with God is necessary. Being released from the feelings of restlessness and rushing is necessary. The Preacher must realize the benefit of establishing a consistent time within the day to connect with God. This will yield the preacher tremendous dividends to more thoughtful and meaningful discovery in scripture. Galileo the great scientist was quoted by John Maxwell as stating that "All truths are easy to understand once they are discovered. The point is to discover them."(Maxwell 2012, 56) As preachers that are prodding for biblical truth there must be a theological curiosity to excavate the challenging and calming truths of God that results in our conformity to Christ.

When we study the Word of God there must be an acknowledgement that spiritual transformation is a necessary goal in our study. Paul Scott Wilson urges us that "As much as the Bible is a historical witness, it is also about us."(Wilson 2004, 1) Unconsciously there can come a time when you are on anointed auto-pilot when you are sermonizing but you have abdicated the spiritual responsibility of preaching that connects with you as much as it makes a connection with the people. This can go unnoticed or under the radar if there's not a smug-less magnifying glass of intentional self-reflection that gives us the significant opportunity for maturation while preparing the message.

Can you deliberately engage in divine down time? As I reflect on engaging down time with God, the image and experience that comes to mind is the directives of the flight attendant on an aircraft. The flight attendant instructs those passengers who are about to experience flight that there is an aviation requirement to turn their devices on airplane mode. When the cellular devices, laptops or tablets are turned on airplane mode there is no signal received, no incoming messages or notifications until you arrive at your destination at which time you can remove it from airplane mode as you are de-boarding. As I observe the best preparatory practice of the preacher, I believe there is a need to swipe toward sermonic airplane mode. As the preacher ascends to receive heavenly impartation there should be no distractive elements or communicative coercion that sidetracks the sermon from collecting invaluable insights from God. These insights that are received while in heavenly places, are useless and meaningless if they are muffled by the mundane when they are proclaim on main street of the human existence.

Studying the Word of God Pluralistically

Self-centered preaching can be done but Christ Centered Preaching is more profitable. Bryan Chapell, in his text *Christ Centered Preaching* challenges the preacher to find God in the text while also expressing the redemptive message and tone in the text. This is what Chapell articulates as the (FCF) Fallen Condition Focus. When Studying God's word for preaching precision it is for an increase in effectiveness, negating the emphasis on the pursuit of personal notoriety as an end unto itself. We are called to a collectivistic consciousness as clergy. O Wesley Allen stated in one of his volumes entitled *Determining the Form* from the series *The Elements of Preaching* that there are two fundamental questions to consider which are vital to preaching a sermon: "What is being said and How it is said". I want to add to these questions another question for you to ponder; Who is receiving what is being said? (Allen 2008, 1)

Preparation is a search for a depth of clarity so that spiritual blindness is removed. If the preacher is intoxicated with his or her own homiletical aroma it will become offensive liken unto those who have applied an abundance of cologne or perfume so that what has a sweet savoring smell is now overpowering. When there is too much of us in a sermon it is overpowering! This is not a license for you to pirate a sermon or adopt the acceptance of a phraseological homiletic felony. We can't allow our objectives for the sermon overpower the purpose for why we stand behind a pulpit in the first place and that is to give diversified access points to find God. The preacher's obscure infatuation for the passage must not tip the scales of his passion for the people. Preachers must love the people. Think it not strange in 1 Corinthians 13 Paul stated I may speak with the tongues of angels but if I don't have love(charity) I am nothing.

The preacher must be in it with the people. He or she must feel the pain of the people; the preacher must have compassion for the condition that the people and himself/herself have found themselves. We have to acknowledge the Sidetracked State of Depravity. (SSD) Everyone has experienced being sidetracked with sinful secondary activity that place us in spiritual poverty. It is very important how we view ourselves as clergy compared and contrasted to how we view those in whom we minister to during the sermonic event. We have an integral responsibility as Moses did to our contemporary Pharaohs and recapitulate the righteous declaration "Let my people Go." This is still our present declaration. Our wholistic freedom is inextricably connected to the obedience of freeing those in whom we serve through the reconciling power of Christ. God has commissioned the gifted to use our gifts, talents, and proclamation of the word of God to empower listeners to seek and claim the deliverance that is availed to them through God.

We should never forget as Thomas Long expressed in his marvelous book *The Witness of Preaching*, that as a witness of heaven we actually came from the congregation as a witness to witnesses. Those who are now bearing witness to what God is doing through you as His chosen witness and have had interaction with you prior to the consecrated transaction. There must not be a fickle forgetfulness that our faith was developed in the midst of the corporate koinonia (fellowship) and we owe a great debt to those who blazed the trail of our own spiritual enlightenment. Therefore, with every opportunity we should joyfully capitalize on cultivating the grounds which we have been freshly removed.

This perspective of ministry can be challenging in an individualistic driven culture. The American dream has applied its tightening grip on the celebrity seeking preacher so that personal advancement has dethrone providential pristine advocacy for those wandering in the wilderness of worthlessness and nihilism. Ted Smith calls this "Star quality" these clergy seek their authority in a consumer culture(where) celebrity has become a powerful, legitimating force used in promotion of both products and ideas. (McClure 2007, 9) We should not convert to the culture when we should be ushering in the receptivity of the kingdom of God. Preachers need not waste countless hours, years and decades climbing the hall of fame ladder of 'preachdom' just to learn it was leaning against the wrong building (Alluding to Sam Chad's book on leadership). Instead we should invest in Kingdom impact and empowerment in God. Karl Barth emphasized "that there was no room for art or method concerning… preaching, or anything that would stand between the Word and the congregation." (Wilson 2004, 114)

As a minister, underestimating your influence can cause colossal cracks in the foundation of congregants' own approach toward preparation. If the people experience an inconsistent spiritual orator deriving from a depleted life of study; this behavior will be indelible duplicated in congregants handling the sacred things of God. People need viable examples to mirror themselves after in ministry. There must not be a gulf between how you are speaking in ministry and what you are showing them in your ministerial character. The concern that some preachers have expressed is the lack of commitment, the negligence and lack of sacrifice for God, the reframing from positioning oneself for an encounter with God. This is the symptom of what Julius Campbell stated to Gerry Bertier in the Motion picture *Remember the Titians* which was that "Attitude reflects leadership captain."

Studying the Word of God Providentially

Where do we find God in our studying! God is so massive and large how could we ever miss God in our time of Study? He is naturally the Motivating Factor (MF) or He should be! God of course is our 'Why' for studying right? Or is He? Whether you prioritize God in your studies speaks volumes about your preaching. Augustine was correct when he stated; "It is hard to proclaim Christ when you don't have a relationship with him." Joseph Ruggles Wilson stated this concerning preaching: "Become what you Preach and then preach Christ in you."

We are warned by Jesus to be on the lookout for those who are infatuated with ministry but have no infiltration of the miraculous power of God's presence. Remember how Jesus expressed in Matthew 7:22 to those following him that God does not turn down free labor. Jesus states, "In that day they will say didn't we prophesy, didn't we preach in your name*, didn't we cast out demons in your name and Jesus says depart from me workers of iniquity I never knew you".

The preacher needs to line themselves up with Lectio Divina. This is an exercise wherein you experience the life changing presence of Christ which is liken unto a quenching waterfall that saturates seekers and soaks them with scriptures which leaves dripping puddles of providential residue that others profit from due to your godly pursuits.

The Matthean community was reminded by Jesus in Matthew 6:33 to Seek first the kingdom of God and His righteousness and all these things shall be added unto you. The premise of this statement is the trust of those who are trailing behind God. That those that are working for God should not endorse worrying as a common practice rather they should have total dependency upon God to give them what they need. This same disposition that is purported to this Matthean community is the challenge for the minister who is giving the message. During our study time with God our trust in God should increase; There should be a reliance, a dependency upon God in our preaching. Just as the sailor positions and sets the sail awaiting the wind to carry it to its destination. The preacher should also open up their theological sail and catch the ruah or the pneuma of God to take the preacher in the designated direction that can change the lives of the people of God. The time will come when our motors of ministerial mastery will fail, the engine of our theological ingenuity will sputter; and our sharp skill will leave us stranded in doctrinal 'No-where's-ville' as struggling neophytes. These are the moments that we have the ills and issues of Ezekiel 37 dried eyes (dry bones) upon dazzling documents, realizing how much we need the instituting empowerment of God to allow the Wind of God's grace to cover us with a whiff of life changing power.

My father always impressed upon me something that I will always remember in my preparation for pulpit proclamation which was, preparation is not just for knowledge of the word alone but also for the direction through the power of the Holy Spirit. This power is irreplaceable in the dynamic of studying. God fills the preacher to the brim reinforcing his/her commitment to remain steady and careful in order to avoid any unnecessary spillage of spiritual impartation that might be caused by any impotent intentionality. After this time of study and we approach the divine moment of preaching we are likened unto Mary with the alabaster box. We too find that there's a designated people that God has ordained that we prepare them for their fleshly burial and spiritual renewal. The oil is not released on the way, it is released when you are in the way and will of God. Never allow those who are not sensitive to the power of God convince you that God is not interested in us giving ourselves to scholarship and spirituality in the study. Archbald T. Roberson says it this way, "Preaching and Scholarship - It is equally true that knowledge does not necessarily prevent one from being a good minister of Jesus but helps him to preach." (Roberson 1890, 9)

Let us ponder this question: Who does Preaching matter to? Let's consider a few categories:

Does it matter to the Preacher as Retiree?

As the preacher walks toward the serene sunset of ministry with the Spring of their ministry now a distant memory (many of whom

I consider to be Mentors), they reflect back to a rearview myriad of riches but also some desires for redactions, edits or changes that they would've made. These preachers now look back over the body of work that has been produced by their homiletic hands. Hands baring marks of what Dr. Marvin McMickle calls, *"The Making of a Preacher."* These clergy's successes were not nurtured through the marketing of news feeds but the byproduct of solemn seeds of strenuous, serious and steady sermonic study and postures of preparation; the marvelous mixture of accomplishments, disappointments, joys and the moments of misery; the Blessit blend of bitter and sweet; the sweet burden of preaching ministry. Looming, there is a pressing question in the backdrop of these clergy's efforts: Does my contribution have a sustainable quality? Or, will it vanish as quick as an echoing oral effect? I'm reminded of the perspective of Adonais Creed in the motion picture Creed II (found in the deleted scenes) which offered some profound insights… In the scene there is an adoring fan taking pictures of Adonais when he turns to his wife nicknamed "Bea" and states "I don't want to be famous but remembered". Preaching Matters to those who are clocking out from Pastoring but plowing still in their Preaching. The question looms… after the beckoning books of faithfulness close, will I be remembered for the service rendered unto God and servitude displayed toward others?

Does it matter to the Preacher that has been Reinstated?

The preacher that emphatically discovers that the grace of God is not revocable, because of the irascible and irrational spiritual decisions they've made in the name of the Lord but are in fact certainly life giving. Preaching Matters to the preacher who has fallen; I mean flat on their face; the preacher who is suicidal because of the dropping of the standard; it matters to the preacher who has bought the basic economy ticket version of the derange rendition of the gospel and who've found that there is no room for any mistakes and you lose all because you failed in one moment of weakness.

Lest it is falsely communicated, I am not an advocate for cheap grace as Fred Craddock refers to an imagery of a watered-down milkshake that is worthless. But there is a primer "grace" that bears similarities to Kroger's rich butter pecan ice cream known as "private selection". We are privately selected by God! In the call narrative of Isaiah 6 the scripture says that it was in the year that King Uzziah died that I saw the Lord high and lifted up and his train filled the temple; or Jeremiah's call narrative that informed us that before you were formed in your mother's womb I knew you; or the account of Rahab that offers an interesting incidental report of her past but God used her. God can use us beyond the scattered sequences of sin that aren't profitable to our souls. It is enormously necessary for us to allow clergy the right to reenter into ministry after an experience of moral failure and who are burdened down and victims of ministerial burn out. Confucius stated "Our greatest glory is not in never falling, but in rising every time we fall."

Does it matter to the Preacher as a Rookie?

The purest time in a preacher's ministry is his or her first sermon and after that he or she is tainted according to Gardener Taylor. Expectations become the order of the day. Most try to fight off or ignore the pulling and the probing of so many that want to compare you; critique you; count you out; or covet what you have. Ministry for the freshly starting preacher is like a pre-mature baby. There is a high level of sensitivity to cross contaminating germs that have to be considered.

Those that carry the gospel of Jesus Christ must know that the gospel works. As I brewed over the pages of that history of preaching entitled *A Legacy of Preaching*, From the Apostles to the Revivalist they spoke about the simple phrases that were mentioned concerning Paul and Preaching which revealed how important it was to the Apostle Paul. Paul's preaching was oriented around the gospel. As Dennis Johnson says "(Paul) prods us toward the goal of perfection not by moving our gaze away from Jesus to other issues but by driving our exploration deeper into Christ" (Forest and King 2018, 38). John Wesley was cited stating to many the importance of urging preachers to use language that was plain, proper and clear. (Duduit 1992, 31) The plague of the young preacher is his/her desire to rise in the ranks instead of raising the conscious of people concerning the resurrected Christ.

Preaching Matters to the novice in ministry because they just desire to love God and to make him happy with the fulfillment of their calling. Preaching Matters because they feel alive when they stand; though their legs are like rubber there's a feeling of running after righteousness; and even though the feeling of untamed butterflies are felt in the pit of their stomach, the caterpillar experiences will allow them to preach with the freedom of those who are no longer grounded or bound by opinions and emojis and that shifts the depth of their self-esteem which clips the purity of their sermonic wings. They focus on the fear of failure oppose to being faithful to an unfailing God.

After contemplating the significance of the oratorical responsibility to communicate God's word, does Preaching Matter? Some would say that the answer is subjective, but I believe that the answer is sovereign! Whatever matters to God in humanity is what should matter to us. Preaching matters to God! First Corinthians 1:18NASV tells us "For the preaching of the cross is to them that perish foolishness; but unto us which are saved it is the power of God." When we know that it matters, we must proceed with a certain manner of handling the gospel with grace and grit that exposes others to His glory. If you believe in the meaningfulness of preaching turn the page and we will examine further why Preaching Matters.

Chapter 2

When Matters Worsen

In January of 2020, the United States had circulating reports involving the spread of a killer virus that was based in China. It was later identified as the coronavirus. At the time this threat seemed far from the borders of the United States. I don't have the adequate amount of time in this text to give a thorough definition and/or description of what this illness truly is nor is this text constructed to deal with its horrific and devastatingly deadly affects but, what I will attempt to reveal is how it has affected homiletics since the rising of its heinous head. One of the unfortunate characteristics of the virus is its ability to infect it's host and withholds symptoms for up to 14 days in some of its victims. Gradually this disease made its way into the United States. The unthinkable began to transpire in our culture. Every major sporting industry; Every Walk-in Restaurant; Every Recreational Center was affected; Schools ranging from K-12 to Universities and Seminaries had to close their doors. The film industry was affected, theatres were forced to close; even the Faith based community was deeply affected, churches were moved to close their doors and forced to stream their services to the public from online platforms.

During this critical time when the virus was most vigorous there were subtle conversations of a quarantine that may be executed to stop the spread of the virus. There was pondering of a possible shut down for two-weeks in which everyone would be advised to remain in their homes and not leave unless you had to purchase essential items like food. Grocery stores during this time appeared as though they were being raided, shelves were empty of items such as bread, paper towel, toilet tissue and cleaning supplies. Products with cleansing agents were now a hot commodity. On social media people began complaining that they were stir crazy and had cabin fever. To worsen matters the government advised people (many of whom thrive in social gatherings) to engage in social distancing.

As all of this was transpiring, I had the opportunity to be on a conference call with one of our Clergy Councils in the city of Detroit. There was a physician that worked for one of the hospitals and for the State of Michigan on the call that made an intriguing statement which stuck with me even in the year 2020 and which also reinforced the necessity of the voice of the preacher. She challenged the pastors and preachers by saying "I understand that you are a trusted voice in the community, the people will listen and believe you before they listen to a licensed and professionally trained healthcare consultant who specializes in the medical field. This healthcare professional ended by impressing upon us that "We need you to use your influence in order to educate and speak to the people." This revealed that even in the midst of this crisis facing the U.S. in unprecedented proportions that PREACHING MATTERS.

A Preacher's Influence

John Maxwell has a famous quote; "Leadership is influence" and I whole heartedly agree. After wrestling with the thought provoking statements that came from this healthcare professional, I've concluded that preaching can be classified as godly influence during this time when many people are experiencing a sense of unsurety; sporadic feelings of ambiguity and paralyzing fear is attempting to smother their faith. Even those religious neophytes that didn't have any interest or knowledge of the church, their hearts were now beginning to open to receive information and revelation. But, just prior to this pandemic the normalcy of their life most likely would have been closed to such a communication.

There are times that I believe that the preacher discounts the influence he/she has. There are also those who just don't desire to acknowledge the level of influence that they possess because they don't desire to have a sense of accountability to providence, peers, or the people they serve. I am reminded of something Charles Barkley (Hall of Fame professional basketball player) stated which was "I am not a Role Model" but yet he is a prominent figure in the public square. Millions of kids desire to do what he used to do. The preacher is supposed to be the ultimate role model of faith. He or she has a fiduciary responsibility and there is a standard of living that we must operate in as examples for saints as well as potential saints that desire and deserve to know the way of righteousness. In 1 Corinthians chapter 11 NASB Paul told those individuals at the church at Corinth "Do as I do, for I am doing as Christ." Lest we forget in the Johannine gospel Jesus is highlighted after engaging in an action of servitude in John 13:15 wherein Jesus impressed upon them "I have set you an example so that you should do as I have done for you" which were acts of servitude.

When we don't grasp the gravity of our influence there are missed opportunities that could have been harnessed even in horrific times. God orchestrates holding patterns in life in order that we can help others have a more intimate walk with God. This is where the potency of preaching draws the power of its ethos!

As the pandemic persisted so many individuals utilized their time binge watching movies. What a glorious opportunity for preachers to influence people to shut off the television and instead utilize their time creating a personal development plan which includes meditating on the Word of God and preparing to engage in online Bible study for their spiritual empowerment and enrichment. Some may say that these binge watchers would never do that. My reply is why not? How do you know? If you never offer them options, they won't even be aware that there are spiritually better choices.

Preachers are responsible for audibly influencing people to create a schedule which includes spending quality time with God and prioritizing time with their family. There are two things this virus has taught America for sure and they are there's power in being still and that the preaching's effectiveness has not perished. The life of an average American citizen is a hustle and bustle lifestyle but, becoming too busy can result in no spiritual substance or productivity and that becomes an issue. Preaching matters in a culture boasting about voiced parity but has ignored sacred syllogisms. Preaching matters because it is a graceful guide through a grueling time when people are seeking the shekinah glory of God. This glory that glistens upon the backdrop of desperation which can be comparable to "scintillating diamonds spread on black velvet" as Abraham Smith would say it. This should be the powerful pictorial of what preaching should be in the midst of despair; welcoming diamonds that have weathered their season of pressure that glisten their best in the toughest of times

Communicating Christ in the Crisis

Preaching is largely about the approach. Sam Chad once stated during a lecture that I was privileged to attend "Never waste a good crisis". I personally believe that clergy are called for *Crisis!* It is during those times of uncertainty that we can provide much needed updates from the Utmost God. It is at this time that what the preacher says matters even more so to people. It wasn't as though their words didn't matter or were spurious prior to the crisis but circumstances have made the people more sensitive to the urgency of hearing what is being proclaimed by the preacher. The preacher must be mindful that when the sermon is well developed, the what and how of the sermon are inseparable in the experience of the hearer as O Wesley Allen Jr. suggest. (Allen 2008, 1)

Discerning the Times

The first step in discerning the times is that we need to properly identify what the crisis is. There are times that we are attempting to preach concerning a crisis and we have not yet identified the source of the crisis. How we determine what the crisis is, is by praying, meditating and reflecting deeply on what the events were that led up to the crisis. In the Old Testament collection of writings there were prophets that gave warnings concerning the impending wrath that was to come if the people of God or their enemies did not cease and desist from their unrighteous behavior.

The second step after we have identified the crisis, we need to see what is analogous or a synonymous to that crisis in scripture. There is certainly nothing new under the sun and if this is happening contemporarily then this has also transpired in the world behind the text. The crisis must be named, it must have a term allocated to it so that you can match it with a term that is used in the Bible. For instance, the coronavirus could be viewed as a plague or some might call it a theodicy. You have to name the crisis. This is a great time for you to have a concordance. Most people have the *Strong's Concordance*.

This book is going to be pivotal in its assistance to you in finding every place that this crisis is located in scripture.

After you find these citations in the scriptures, it is vital that we then go through the list rendered by Strong's in a Study Bible that also has commentary at the bottom. The Harper Collins New Revised Standard Version Bible endorsed by the Society of Biblical Literature is excellent. During the time that we are researching these particular texts we will be seeking to find what is the historical and literary context of the text. These selected scriptures that will be used as cross references must be thoroughly examined.

This process reminds me of an experience I had in a Kroger Supermarket where I had a wonderful conversation with a person whom I discovered was a Baptist turned Seventh-day Adventist. The lady handed me a piece of paper that had all types of scriptures about the end of time. The question raised automatically in my mind was that of the doctrine of eschatology (the doctrine of the last things). The paper listed several scriptures but what was the significance of the time period of each and what should be considered or what was the scenario specific to the text? Were there liberties of allegorical interpretation at work in the selection process of these text? In a circumstance such as this, accuracy matters in preaching or the witness of the word!

This glaring example reveals how careful we must be when we are grasping terms from the bible in some unconsciously reckless manner, this might leave people even more confused than they were prior to.

This causes further damage to the ethos of your proclamation. The Study Bible will assist in giving you commentary and introductory information that will quickly paint the landscape of the scenarios that were taking place in antiquity. This small step is a huge step in the interpreter's accuracy in interpretation.

The third step is to find a text that really speaks to the details of what your homiletic dialogue or conversation will convey. This is where Bryan Chapell's Fallen Condition Focus allows us to remain in contact on the passage or Paul Scott Wilson's Major Concern makes us ask the question what is God doing here or what is God's involvement? We could possibly refer to it as **The Revelation of Retrieval of the Text**. How and What did God do to retrieve humanity from this rotten condition? After we have identified how God is involved; there is a need to come up with a working phrase which develops the sermons surrounding structure. This is called the proposition or the Sermonic Claim. Haddon Robinson Big Idea; Samuel Proctors Proposition or Marvin McMickle's Sermonic Claim. This phrase is important and must be considered when you are dealing with a major crisis. We should not consult a major text and excavate minor points. There is so much information that will demand your attention, but you must be discipline enough to know that you cannot sufficiently articulate everything in just a 30 to 45-minute window. There must be what I call selective exegesis. There are certain things that I have excavated from a particular text but, I need to take the components of that exegesis and I need to present them in a form of time release.

Stages of the Crisis

When we engage in preaching while encountering a crisis, we have to discern what stage our congregation is in at the present time and how the world is presently handling the crisis. In an effort to elaborate further, below you'll find three categories that I will expound on: Breaking News, Casual News and Old News.

Breaking News

When a crisis is ramping up every news outlet desires to be the first to report what is transpiring be it TMZ, the national or local news or social media feeds. Depending on how many days this is away from the next service, congregant's minds are being bombarded with tons of information and most of the information is maliciously market driven. There is always someone that is attempting to get paid from someone else's pain. This reminds me of the Woman with the issue of blood and Jairus in Mark 5. The woman went to physicians and spent all she had but she did not get better, but she grew worst. In the interconnected story of Jairus there are professional mourners that are present at the house and they are being paid for their mourning. All because someone is getting paid from someone else's pain does not mean that it is, in the words of Donald Trump, "fake news". It can mean that people are using the unknown factors of ravaging phobia in order to strong arm or increase their profit lines instead of expressing a decency and genuine concern for people.

As preachers of the gospel, we can demonstrate that even in the midst of a crisis our main assignment is our love for God's agenda and the advancement of all people spiritually and sociologically. It is necessary for the preacher to be informed. In the past people used to say that the preacher needed a Bible in one hand and the newspaper in the other but, times have changed tremendously. We need to have the Bible in one hand, the news feed in the other hand and the latest live feed on our laps. We need to be aware of what is coming through the waves and are they in alignment with the word that we are proclaiming. Dr. Farmer stated on one occasion that we have competitive commitments. This means that people have options where they will spend their time. This is also true concerning their desired choice of listening and what particular voices that will ultimately influence their action. Whose voice is louder in the culture? This is not a question or an argument for more volume but what infects us with homiletic laryngitis is lacking enough voice (clarity in thought) in valuable moments of struggle. It is the substance and the Spirit that is in our preaching that will speak volumes to the soul of men, women, millennials and other generational groups and will captivate their attention because our communication is not slanted toward consumerism but leads to introspection which can cause us to move toward reflective measures spiritually instead of being in a constant state of reaction.

Casual News

Prior to the Coronavirus outbreak the news of the untimely death of Kobe Bryant was broadcasted everywhere! Sports fans and entrepreneurs across the globe were devastated by the news of Bryant's death and his precious daughter Gianna Bryant along with seven others in a helicopter crash. As the coronavirus ramped up, the reporting on Bryant was converted into causal news (for the majority of the public anyway). Instead of basketball players being affected by the death of a colleague they were now having to deal with being infected by a virus that suspended the entire NBA Season.

When the preacher issues proclamations in the midst of a crisis that transitions into casual news there is no need to bombard hearers with aimless memories of the miserable events. The better homiletic approach is to give emphasis to a set of biblical principles which provides all with a transformative life plan. This ultimately yields future benefits as well for the people if a similar crisis returns. How tragic would it be to find ourselves at the same stage of maturity that we were prior to the first encounter with the pandemic or crisis. This area of proclamation should be geared toward the pathos with a connection with logos (Emotion=pathos and Intellect=logos). How can we do this effectively? How can we have series of sermons that cover a couple of specific areas?

First there would be sermons surrounding thanksgiving for the deliverance from the crisis. Bishop Edgar Vann in his Masters'

Class taught us that we need to celebrate small victories along the way. This is necessary as the heavy loads are being lifted at each stage. We must learn to preach in the vein of emotional and logical progress. The second area may involve the ways in which we can handle the woundedness from the crisis. There are times that people are physiologically okay but unmarked psychological damage has occurred which has lingering effects. We must walk with them through scriptures that are assuring because they must establish trust again while reminding them to never place their trust in what has failed.

The preacher must be conscious that all because the crisis has subsided, they are nowhere near out of the woods yet. There undoubtedly will be lingering questions and concerns and scares, this is part of the process as we begin the work of embracing the new norm. This brings us to the final stage of how we can handle crisis with effective preaching:

Old News

After the crisis begins to subside and we are confident that it has passed, most people will return to business as usual. This can be analogous to a person that has suffered a heart attack and is not in any immediate danger of losing their life or a person with diabetes that awakens from the diabetic coma but after they've survived and recovered they choose to return back to the life style that placed them in this compromising state to begin with. It is at this stage,

"Old News" wherein we find the need to move from Pathos (what I feel) to Logos (how I think) to Ethos (the integrity of God). When our emotions get the best of us it allows us to engage in a powerful pause for reflection. Lastly, receive fulfillment through examining the integrity of God that fulfills the promises of God. This type of preaching is informative and inspirational; it infiltrates the individual which allows for lasting changes beyond the circumstances.

When we adopt the disposition of remaining aggressively transformative following this Old News-cycle, we can endorse Spiritual Transformation. If you need a guide to aide you in your execution of this, Richard Foster's *Celebration of Discipline* is a tremendous text and reference that you can use to assist the people on the road to spiritual transformation. This area speaks to the logos of the person, the logic. The mind of the person must change which is connected to the heart of the person. This is why Paul says that "I beseech you therefore brethren by the mercies of God that you present your bodies a living sacrifice, holy and acceptable unto God which is your reasonable service and do not conform to this world but be ye transformed by the renewing of your mind". Romans 12:1-2

After the casual news moves to old news, we need to use Spiritual Transformation as a tool in order to create a new normal. Preaching should move from speaking only about the things that transpired in the negative sense to strategically communicating how God delivered us with a mighty hand. Because of the deliverance that has taken place, there is a new course of action; a new place of priorities that need to be endorsed and implemented. The scriptures speak about returning; or changing; or transforming from stony hearts to a heart of flesh. All of these side effects of the former things that the people had to endure are incentives for them to develop an allegiance that is unshakable and a devotion that is unwavering.

Preaching Matters in this sense, oftentimes the preacher possesses the influence to persuade the people to press towards doing something unprecedented even in these moments. This is how lasting movements are created. Individuals become fed up with what transpired and are moved to engage in activities that will literally change the fabric of future generations. Spiritual transformation is allowing old news to become good news especially for those that receive words of wisdom and make the decision to never return back to the mindset of selling themselves cheap but embraces the fact that they are precious in the sight of God resulting in the decision to no longer waste precious time on things that yield no fruit. The responsibilities of the preacher are unique. A reporter only chases breaking news; the journalist can do comparisons and contrast of casual news and breaking news, but the Preacher takes the Breaking News, Casual News, and Old News and then turn them into Good News.

There is one more aspect of proclamation that I would like for you to ponder and that is the crisis of Jesus death. Think about this breaking news, Jesus of Nazareth is being crucified. The news of his crucifixion is sweeping through the unsettled dusty streets of Jerusalem. The news is that out of those who followed him nine are missing, one denied him, one betrayed him and there is only one lone disciple John that is among the observers taking care of his weeping mother. How do we handle the crisis that God is dying! There is no bigger crisis in the world than this. This is truly the unthinkable, but it was newsworthy because Jesus told them this would happen. For three days they are challenged with different stories. By the time the disciples are spoken to they're hearing that the news feeds are saying that they stole the body. Some say Peter came to the tomb and only saw his grave clothes; and what about those who were not in the inner circle that were on their way to Emmaus that are mentioned in the introduction of this text who say they saw him? Also, we cannot forget about those preaching women that said he died one Friday but he got up! It was a total moment of hysteria! Instead of them wondering where is Waldo, they are engage in wondering where is Jesus. Each one of these steps; Breaking News, Casual News and Old News is present in this story.

In this postmodern society this story is considered to be old news. There are those who believe there's a new order of the day, believing the miracles that Jesus performed can now be explained away by science. They even arrogantly believe that humanity is on Jesus' heels and giving Him a run for His money. They have the egregious gall to think sooner or later they'll become the new record holder in the Guinness Book of Worlds Records for an individual Walking on Water. What I find most disturbing is not that the world treats this news as if it were old news but that those in the church and are considered to be a part of the *ekklessia* believe the same. They too have begun treating the death burial and resurrection as though it's old news. Does the Calvary event need an ios update? (Apple software update for phones, computers and tablets) Does it seem as though it's no longer relevant enough to go pound for pound with the technological breakthroughs of this world? As Paul would say "Of course not"! These individuals fail to remember the Y2K Black out that left America in the dark and technology crippled and disabled while Jesus still reigned. The Church is sometimes placed into a state of persecution so that it takes old news and turn it into sustaining good news for the Church. I am a firm believer that the Church with the Preacher as her catalyst has much more to say from the Pulpit but, how to say it has become the challenge. There are several matters in our world today whereby we need to know what side does the church land on. It is through the voice of the Preacher where we learn what God says concerning these things. This is a constant reminder that no matter in what areas we've seen growth in society and no matter it's advancements, it must still resort back to the tour guide of the times, the one in whom God has entrusted with His voice, the preacher. Preaching does Matter especially when crisis smacks humanity in the face with a cold dose of reality.

Chapter 3

What's the Matter with You?

As I reflect back on my earlier years spent in grammar school, I realize that these were some of the most caring years I've experienced in an academic setting. There was a climate of cohesiveness, a joint collaborative effort and a real sense of community. These previously mentioned characteristics were especially sympathetically embossed upon classmates who were having challenging days. The student's whose countenance may have been augmented because of a mild sickness, a domestic disturbance of some sort or a mark on their report card that was not up to par. Even as children we could pick up on their nonverbal communication, sensing that something was not quite right, and we inquired with the interrogative, What's the matter with you?

The preacher that is equipped to handle the highs and lows of life and who masters bringing them into sermonic balance will be the preacher that engross him or herself in learning how to respond with sensitivity and spirituality; one that will go beyond a judgmental inquiry to ask those among him or her "what is the matter?" The truth of the matter is, we find ourselves at a disadvantage when we don't take time to carefully consider the gravity and honest answers that reverberates from the inner recesses of their hearts and ours.

There is a passage of scripture that gets to the heart of the question. Luke chapter 4 provides a careful analysis of what matters are at hand. It is in this passage we see the daily suffering of humanity and how those matters can be adequately addressed. Just Preach the word! Luke 4:18-19 KJV The Spirit of the Lord is upon me, because he hath anointed me to preach the gospel to the poor ; he hath sent me to heal the brokenhearted, to preach deliverance to the captives, and recovering of sight to the blind, to set at liberty them that are bruised, to preach the acceptable year of the Lord.

This matter is spotlighted in what the *Hermeneia* refers to, the First Public Preaching in Nazareth. (Francois 2002, 148) This preaching of Jesus reveals that it was/is through his speeches and miracles that the inner core of a person can be reached even now. The centerpiece, the nucleus, and the hedge that holds steady these heavenly statements is Preaching. The matters voiced in the passage was met with the practical revelation that Preaching does matter to the humane situation. It further reveals that preaching captivates the intrinsic features necessary to cultivate, capture and usher in a drastic change for those that lay under the Grace Filled Weight of the preaching of the gospel. Jesus' preaching mattered because he dealt with specific areas that mattered to those in whom he was anointed to minister to. He addressed their agonies and alleviated them accordingly.

Preaching in Luke 4:18-19 is almost laced through every line, which bespeaks its essential nature. The inaugural term for preaching and the one that will be sustained throughout this pericope in this address given by Jesus to the anxious audience was keryxai which is a verb. It means to make an announcement; to herald; or to proclaim. Here the word preaching (the verb) reveals its activity but also the effects of preaching whether it be in the present or in the future. Preaching matters because the effects of it transcends space and time of the sermonic event. It lives in the corridors that the preacher will never travel physically. These words remain as potent as they were when they were first uttered just as we still feel the presence of God today. These divine utterances that are spiritually transacted through us are by no means because of our celestial skill or our ability to craft glorious syntactical combinations but it is because the authority of God rest upon our feeble attempts. This makes them tasteful to the spiritual palate or textual taste buds, oppose to having an immediate expiration post the preaching expression.

Now that we have examined preaching briefly from an etymological place let us consider the matters that preaching addresses in this textual construct. The first category addressed is the poor. The poor are those who are dependent upon others support. There is a state of dependence that the poor are characterized by! Those who are not self-sustained or self-sufficient, this virtually speaks to those who have need for assistance and can actually admit that they are in need of it. I believe that it is amazing that we find in Matthew, the 5th chapter what is frequently referred to in the ecclesiastical sector "the Be Attitudes" or what some refer to under the theological subheading "The Sermon on the Mount". Most scholars point out the mention of the poor was the very first thing that Jesus addressed, he stated "blessed are the poor in spirit." Matthew 5:3 NASB!

This reveals that poverty is not always viewed in a negative light. It is a prism type of phonics that depending upon the way that you turn it, it reveals its luster from a variety of angles. Here when it says blessed are the poor in spirit in the 5th Chapter of Matthew up until the final verse in chapter 6 it's dealing with the spiritual responsibility to seeking first the kingdom of God and its righteousness.

There are several instances that Jesus illumines wherein He grants the blessing to those that have total dependence on God. These happy individuals are those who will not allow for worry to infiltrate their person because their faith reminds them that their wealth is in the assistance of God. So, Jesus speaks of those who are poor in spirit to make a distinct contrast to those who are rich in spirit. Contrary to those that are dependent on God, these individuals think they are self-sufficient and that they aren't in need of assistance from the kingdom. The rich in spirit believe that they can manage the things in life on their own. Jesus gives commendations not to the latter group but the former group when he admonished them in Matthew 6:33 that if you keep me first I will add the other things that you may believe that you are losing out on.

Preaching matters to those who are poor because it informs them that they are not restricted. Those who find themselves in disparity definitely don't have to resort to dealing with this world in an individualistic manner. We have a guarantee that when we follow godly principles the Lord will support them by sending the very best that he had in the personality of Christ.

The second mentionable highlighted in the text was to the captives.

These are those individuals that are prisoners in one form or another. During one of my first trips to the Academy of Homiletics, I had the pleasure of having dinner with one of my mentors. During our time together, we engaged in thought-provoking dialogue concerning academia and how it is wedded with the ecclesiastical. As we spoke about how the church needs to be more sensitive toward social issues and the impact it has on those who attend church, some powerful points emerged. In the book entitled the New Jim crow by Michelle Alexander, she shines a spotlight on the incarceration system and how it stands front and center as a systemic entity to perpetuate former discriminatory practices in new ways. My mentor further explained how so many aren't interested in prison ministry although this very ministry is saturated in the Book of Acts along with other various forms of incarceration.

When we research the scriptures, we discover that incarceration led to most of the letters that we now declare as canon. Preaching that matters must deal with the incarceration issues of the physiological, sociologically, economically, racial and definitely the soul of man. Does preaching matter to those who are captive in these systems? I believe it does! Those who are in the system need a form of communication that leads them to healthy solutions and releases them to the authenticity of operating in the world as a viable believer detached from a chained consciousness because of the liberating message that preaching provides. Rev. Al Sharpton describes it as a knee on your neck prophetically citing the murder of George Floyd.

The next category mentioned is the giving sight to the blind.

The word blind here deals with the lack of sight but, it also can be viewed as having a lack of comprehension. After tracing the gospel and tracking all of the miracles, one of the most reoccurring miracles is Jesus giving sight to the blind. According to scholars who examined these occurrences, they mirror the activity of Jesus' interaction with his disciples. How about that blind man in Mark 8:4 NASB who Jesus touched twice because when he touched him the first time he could only see men as trees but then the second touch, he than could see clearly. This was a representation of the disciples not being able to consistently see clearly. They saw in faith but then doubt would blind them again. The second story that can be referenced is in Mark 10:46-52 when blind Bartimaeus shouted "Son of David have mercy on me". If you recall, prior to this episodic encounter some of the disciples are having a conversation concerning who is the greatest in the kingdom and where they should sit. Abraham Smith stated that they wanted seats and Bartimaeus desired sight! The very thing that Bartimaeus had the disciples should have desired to have which is spiritual insight.

Preaching Matters in this particular area because it informs us of our blind spots. Our world is plagued with those in high places and low positions but, they are unable to see. Their blindness causes confusion. Does preaching matter to those who are blind? Blind to their racial bigotry; blind to their homophobic inclinations of harbored hate opposed to a health holy critique; blind to their economical privilege or blind to how ecclesiastically wrapped in genderism and misogynistic privilege in the pulpit and the pew they are. Martin Luther king said injustice anywhere is injustice everywhere. I believe preaching matters to those that can have an allying voice of advocacy that can sway the tides of tension to place cataract cancelling door stoppers in the path of those who desire to perpetuate these deem dispositions.

Preaching needs to be action oriented

While listening to one of my favorite preachers Joel Gregory, he recited a quote of someone who said, "The issue with people is that their audio does not match their video and what was being sad did not match what was being done." This is one of the reasons I believe that people will caricature, negatively and aggressively respond to religious rhetoric. Does Preaching matter? It is tough for people to answer in the affirmative when the audio does not match with the video.

When social media has become a snake pit of strange activity. There is no shortage of groping, guzzling down strange spirits, bragging about their ministerial mouths proudly descending below mid-sections of congregants who are supposed to be receiving the preached message; but instead are being saturated with the spirit they choose. All of these demonic devices are weapons of seduction used in an attempt to muffle the miraculous message of Christ because their video doesn't match their audio.

There is a personal experience that has been securely filed away in my memory from my childhood of when I was attending the Courtis Elementary School Library. We had the opportunity to watch the movie *Roots*, but it was in a very different format than 4K or Ultra Blu-ray. There was a projector and a handheld tape recorder that produced the sound. When the beep in the recording sounded the person that was responsible for transitioning the slides had the responsibility of pressing the button to change the slides. If that someone was goofing-off they would miss the beep and the scene that was presently on the screen would be totally different from what was being stated on the audio. The video did not match the audio. This is a homiletic lesson for all of those who are committed to clearly communicating the gospel with precision. Don't ignore or miss the beep of the Holy Spirit! There are impromptu imports that we mustn't ignore because of impatience but it is the job of the preacher to give themselves over to the impeccable impact of the speaking of the Holy Spirit. Preaching matters when we can use the transformative qualities of the word of God to help them acknowledge their Sidetrack State of Depravity (SSD). If we don't feel the weight of this responsibility, we must access if preaching really matter to us!

When Preaching Matters to you there's an enthusiastic quality to your preaching. Zig Ziglar reminds us that enthusiasm is not being loud, but according to Zig it comes from two Greek words that means "in God". He says enthusiasm centrality is in the ism of the word and that is "I'm sold myself." When you are convinced that the message that was preached has helped you in the mundane matters of this world you can't help but share what the Lord has given you because you desire for others to enjoy the experience that you just had.

What is the Matter with You? From Another View

A popular movie series that has stood the test of time and has become an all-time classic is Silvester Stallone's Rocky Series. One of the most interesting among the series is when Rocky loses his trainer to a heart attack. Shortly after he loses his title to Clubber Lane, portrayed by Mr. T.

During the time of the fight, standing ring side was the former champion and former rival Apollo Creed. He witnessed the utter destruction of Rocky under the glistering lights by Clubber Lane. Apollo was disappointed in what he was witnessing as he recalled when Rocky fought him years earlier, he was different, untamed, and unorthodox. Desiring to see Rocky return mentally to his former glory, he offered to train Rocky in a new way hoping to couple his former mindset which enabled him to win with a more formal training. Formerly, Rocky's boxing was a flat-footed southpaw that was more bruiser than boxer. Apollo was attempting to show Rocky how to fight in a different way which would make him faster if he stayed on his toes and did more jabbing.

There is a very intriguing scene where during one his training sessions with Apollo, Rocky appears to give in to defeat because he keeps rehearsing in his mind the loss of his manger and visions of being punched in his head and eventually knocked out by Clubber Lane. At one point he just stopped running and Apollo begins screaming at him, "What is the Matter with you?"

The purpose behind the question was to bring attention to the fact that he was not acting like the same fighter that he was when he had previously beat Apollo which also led to his becoming champion. At that time, he possessed will and determination and was relentless. He had become known for his bounce back, fight back and attack but, it appeared as though it all seemed to have vanquished. This line of interrogation isn't just a great line spoken from the mouth of an actor, but it is a question that is spoken from the throne of God. What is the matter with you?

I believe that we can contextualize this question drawing from the biblical writ in the book of Kings 19:13, Elijah the prophet has a threat that looms over his head from Jezebel and finds himself depressed with his faith dissolving in a dusty cave. God asked him this question, "What are you doing here Elijah?" (WHAT IS THE MATTER WITH YOU) All that God had previously done through Elijah such as; appearing to lock up and putting on strike the liquidity of water droplets until Elijah uses the linguistic "Let it rain"; or Elijah's calling down fire from the firmaments to expose the falsities of those who depend on polytheisms. Now because of a threat from Jezebel he's allowed all of that passion and preaching to dissipate, and it has landed him in a dusty dingy domain. A cave!

During my reading of a homiletic journal from the Academy of Homiletics, I discovered an interesting take on Elijah's ministry especially in 1 Kings 17. Elijah's pronouncement was delineated as his trial sermon so to speak and from that point we saw the evolving of Elijah who became a spectacular prophet. There are times in the life of the preacher wherein transformation occurs. Adjustments in ministry are inevitable but the adjustments that are made must be appropriate and in alignment with where the Lord is taking you. There are three areas wherein we must proceed with caution so that we don't lose what Apollo describes as the eye of the tiger in ministry.

Building Barnes and Starving Souls

We must be careful not to get entrenched in this super stardom and celebrity syndrome that comes with megachurch fever. It is very easy to start building for a personal legacy and forget all about the original calling that God has placed over your life. Many ministers have fallen casualty to this mindset in ministry because they've lost sight of what is important. There are those that desire multi campus ministries and unfortunately this might have exclusively perpetuated the mindset of building barns instead of building churches. It is actually a barn that we have planted a steeple on top of.

Luke 12:16-20 There was a rich man that yielded an abundance of crops and he thought to himself, "What shall I do? I have no place to store my crops." Then he said, "This is what I'll do. I will tear down my barns and build bigger ones, and there I will store my surplus grain and I'll say to myself, you have plenty of grain laid up for many years, take life easy, eat, drink and be merry." But God said to him, "You fool, this very night your life will be demanded from you. Then who will get what you have prepared for yourself?"

This man is a great example of any preacher that is building their kingdom opposed to building the kingdom of God. This is not to suggest that every Pastor that has multiple church campuses is not building for God. But, if it is not being done through obedience and to the glory of God but to brag and to glory in your own name then it isn't a church any longer, they are barns with steeples. It behooves the pastor that is having success in harvesting souls to remain humble and to exercise care that they don't choose to have selective amnesia concerning the one that is blessing the work of their hands

Theatrics Instead of Theology

The second temptation that we have to refute is becoming performers. In that wonderful book *"Leaders That Last"* by Alfred Ells and Gary Kinnamen, there's one pastor says that I feel like a circus monkey and that they're awaiting my performance each week. This reflects the sentiment of many. There are those who are chasing the false notion that you can preach a great sermon every Sunday. First, we must define what meets the requirement of being called a great sermon. In this day and time unfortunately, everything is labeled great. There are no real standards that we can compare greatness to or a set barometer for greatness.

We have to be careful about a performance that is bent on people pleasing. My father used to say that one of his instructors, Dr. Evans taught the seminarians that "It is not about making people feel good, but the objective is for the people to be good." When people are the center of your congratulatory focus following the proclamation of God's word, we will go to any length in order that we can hear those affirmations from our audience. This was why John Chrysostom stopped individuals from responding to his sermons because he desired to be indifferent to praise!

There are those who rather see theatre than to hear sound theology. They crave for crumbling theological crackerjacks that are sweet to the congregant's taste buds but bitter to the betterment of their soul. Being theological means that you are making a conscious effort to allow the authors intent to be your leading premise in your preaching. It breaks my heart when people tell other people that if you desire to learn Hebrew and Greek then just google it. The purpose of Hebrew and Greek is to grant clarity of understanding of that which is being conveyed in the past so that it can impact the hearers view of the scriptures which places it in the proper context. Phonetic gymnastics of empty declarations that only work in the church but aren't revealed in crisis won't help the church. It causes a theological induced coma which leads to our engaging in a prelude of administering Novocain for their pain. This is done in an effort to rid them of the pain of their present realities opposed to giving them the tools to fight with, their faith. We don't need clowns and or satanic bipolar jokers, we need clergy that will preacher with conviction and power!

Don't get your homiletical hands dirty!

The last temptation that we need to be aware of is, not allowing for you to lose who you are in ministry. There are those preachers that begin with promissory notes of greatness that could certainly yield dividends in the future but unfortunately, they allow for the wrong influences to distract and even destroy their future. One concept that has swept across the country is individuals that are attempting to blend philosophy, rhetoric and ancient religious beliefs, all of which they have not researched nor have fully understood. This irresponsibility has created unnecessary friction in the body of Christ. Les brown says that "Faith is the oil that takes the friction out life." Well our preaching ought to be the oil that offer relief to people and helps them avoid the friction of theological confusion. There are those that believe because they have a national ministry and they're in high demand that this affords them the permission to verbalize careless theological jargon. They feel as though if they don't "say it here" there are 20 churches that are waiting to take their spot.

As of late, I have unfortunately seen prominent pastors and preachers whom in the earlier years of their ministry left and went astray to theological heresy. They are stating there is no hell and that there is another way to God outside of Jesus Christ. This is disturbing to say the least because they started out stating that there was a Hell and that Jesus is the only way but have succumbed to the pressing movements in their churches, the pressing culture as though God is evolving. They have unfortunately fallen prey to these heretical thoughts. There are times that we are too deep and if not for the grace of God we would've fallen off the deep in. So many say in today's society that we should use common sense, but everything that is in and of God does not make sense to man.

I believe that there is a need for us to grasp hold to unfaltering humility. This will allow us to focus our attention on what God desires to do in our lives. God is asking right now in some of your lives, "What is the Matter with you?" What used to convict you doesn't.... "What is the matter with you?" What used to bring you joy doesn't... "What is the matter with you?" The gift of proclaiming God's word was meant to give life but now you are pondering taking your own life... "What is the matter with you?" We all need a preacher to perform diagnostics because we have lights signaling that something is out of whack and that we need to be reminded to place our affections toward those things in God which really matter.

As we wrap up this chapter, I'll never forget my elementary experiences and the inquisitive questions we asked, one of which has stuck with me down through the years and that is 'What's the matter?' This question was asked because the person authentically cared. It is my earnest desire for the world, this nation, communities in American culture, community groups and most definitely churches to be concerned enough to ask, what is the matter? We must express to those who have received the inquiry that at the heart of the organization's ontological make-up, it is genuinely concerned about what happens to them and others.

The world needs a download, an air drop of compassion. There are those among us who are suffering from societal pressures that are smothering their emotional and moral sensitivity. People are sensitive concerning being politically correct but, that sensitivity needs to extend towards pursuing potent antidotes to pertinent problems impacting people psychologically and ultimately spiritually.

In times like these we need a Savior; In times like these we need an anchor to grip the Solid Rock. That Rock is Jesus!

Chapter 4

Taking Matters into your Own Hands

There is a radical responsibility in preaching. Clerics must remain mindful that "If preachers are inconsistent in voice, the gospel is represented as being incoherent." In this existing ecclesiastical culture, there is apparently a race for pulpit status, it is evident that there is little understanding of the true essence of the reality of what it means to be a preacher, let alone to preach. Discerning the gravity, the depth of responsibility and level of sacrifice that it entails for a person to enter into the sacred office of the preacher is being neglected and ignored by perfunctory ambitions. Woe to those who don't have a reverential holy hesitation. Woe to those who don't give a pregnant second thought. They dive with serendipitous inclinations into divine matters. But eventually, these, by chance clergy (called by chance) find themselves homiletically drowning. The extremity of commitment to preaching excellence is not offered on the shallow end of ministerial life.

Preaching nowadays has gone viral. Preaching is trending.

Everyone has cameras everywhere attempting to catch soundbites or a moment that can be used for marketing. Preachers have a participatory responsibility in this because they have conformed to the model of celebrity access while being mic'd up, embracing the reality show personae as a suitable element which has crept into the framework of the responsibilities of ministry. They have high camera phone usage but low commitment to Christ's philanthropy and focus. We are living in a time where even the minister has bought into the hype of taking selfies prior to the moment of proclamation and using the phraseology "pray for the preacher." I have always wondered how preachers have the time to even think about taking a selfie while contemplating the immense chasm between sinners and the savior Jesus Christ. Not to mention the weight of the sermon alone which can easily be suffocated by the smallest distractions formed by Satan to nullify the importance of the preaching moment. Maybe they believe that they are god's gift to preaching, instead of preaching being a gift to them.

There are various theological views and models concerning the role of the minister and those who engage in the ministering of God's word. In some traditions everyone is a minister and they can extemporaneously receive a beckoning from the pulpit to come to the podium and give a 5 to 10-minute talk (word). This is constituted as the ministry of all believers. In my humble prospective of preaching there is a sense of calling. An experience that transpires in the head and heart of the individual that is divinely appointed. There is a nagging nudge; there is an *"involuntary imprisonment"* as Terry Wardle would call it, a strange air of the unknown that you sense deeply. It is problematic to capture the colossal nature of "the call" in a solid sentence. Mother Teresa calls it a "call within the call" The old adage is appropriate here and that is it takes one to know one!

Marvin McMickle eludes to this sense of calling in his masterful written text *The Making of a Preacher.* He uses the call narrative of Moses as a prototype of what the minister has to endure and encounter in order that he/she might fulfill this sense of calling over their lives. There is no simplicity in the nature of the calling to minister to the people of God.

The Weight of Waiting

Frequently ministers retract from conditions which demand a waiting period. As the preacher takes the embryonic journey of ministry, they will acquaint themselves with the reality that there is a period of isolation for preparation. This period of ordained pausing transpires no matter how prolific you are. Stillness is a part of the Sovereign strategy no matter what stage you are currently in ministry. If there was anyone that you thought would come out of the box assembled, it would have been Saul who is now converted to be the Pauline Personality. If you want to see a listing of all the peerless accessories that Paul had, you can read the list in Philippians 3:5.

In spite of all that Paul possessed there was a phase when he had to submit under the weight of waiting. This weight is tough for some preachers to handle as you introspectively reflect on the gifting that you possess; you believe I'm too gifted to be held hostage buy being placed on hold. There are times that the minister must wait because there are myopic immaturities and ministerial babyhoods that are still present that are not as pronounced or perceptible on the surface. There are challenges and circumstances that bring to the surface those concealed character flaws.

During my early stages of seminary education, we had to take out time to write a Philosophy of Ministry. In this exercise people expediently wrote down things that they desired to complete and items they craved to accomplish in ministry. This paper is never assigned for that purpose. This exercise exposes the inner core of the person. This particular paper is devised to inform you of the depth of your purpose as a preacher. It is not focused on *doing* but instead on *being*. It is quite possible that when we go into ministry we struggle initially because we have not the process recklessly reversed. We believe that we are supposed to begin performing ministry for the people, when we should be acquainting ourselves with God to find out how he has made us; what he has made us for; who he has made us to be and when has he decided for us to use what he placed in us.

What will the weight of waiting offer to you as a preacher?

- **Original source of Pouring**
- **Assistance from Awkward Places**
- **Volunteers that Vouch for you**

♦ Complexity that develop into Profound Simplicity

When Paul waited he had the opportunity to receive pouring from Jesus himself, the **Original Source of Pouring**. Paul had a ministry that was stamped with originality. Paul of course, has been credited with the domestic dictation of divine oracles. But there are others that become trapped in the euphemism of other's images, like a key incorrectly cut. This brings to mind a story E.L. Branch tells about a copy of the house key he gave to his daughter that malfunctioned. He thought the key was cut incorrectly but discovered that because he had duplicated the copy of the key for so long it no longer worked. The advice of the locksmith was that in order for the key to work correctly, he needed to go back to the original. I believe the same can be said about preaching and that is, in order to make preaching tremendously powerful in our day and time, we need to go back to the original(Jesus) and seek the way Jesus proclaimed the word of God.

According to Scriptures after time had passed Paul was visited by Ananias who touched him, and the biblical writ records that it was like scales that fell from his eyes Acts 9:17 NRSV. This was an **Awkward Assistance** because Ananias did not desire to touch Saul. There was trepidation in Ananias because of the history of this man who persecuted the church. During the waiting period God will dispatch those who are disaffected with the direction that you have been taking and their interruption will remove the scales from your eyes. There are people who you may consider antithesis for the direction of your ministry but, they will offer fresh perspective to your experience of ministerial life.

Volunteers that will vouch for you – These are the Barnabas's that come to your aid. Barnabas is the son of encouragement. There are those that will give exposure to your gift and open doors that your former character has closed. Barnabas is an embodiment of Grace, the places that we don't deserve to be a part of; the settings that would have continued to silence us. Barnabas is the grace necessary to allow you to move beyond where you are currently and give you the opportunity through intentional exposure. This will make you say nobody but God!

Complexity that turns into profound Simplicity - Paul was very academically astute but he said that he developed his arguments in such a meticulous fashion that he made the profound things of God simple. Being simple minded and knowing how to transform to simplicity from depths of thought takes a lot of intentional measures. Paul stated that "Lest I empty the cross of its power I did not come with eloquence or speech that was top heavy."

There has been a trade off from the weight of waiting to focusing on what we are wearing, especially in North America. Ministry has become a fashion statement. It is dangerous for you to look "preachy" but, you don't know how to preach. The rule of thumb is that your wardrobe should not be more expensive than the word that is coming out of your mouth. My father used to tell me with regularity that books buy suits, suits don't by books. He told me this so that I would prioritized my ministry over materialism. During developmental years as a youngster in the faith, there was a high reverence for the man or woman of the cloth. They were distinguished men and women. They presented themselves in a way that demanded respect and that showcased who they represented but now we have seen a condescending to garments that make us look like commoners instead of communicators called by Christ. I am not suggesting the flare and the flash to draw attention to yourself but that your mindset should be to dress appropriately and in a way that leaves no doubt to the question of what does your style appear to be selling?

Control What You Can Control

Oftentimes a phrase comes to my mind that offered by my older brother affectionately known as "J"! He says, "All you can control is your attitude and your activity." He further explained to me, "Control what you can control because that is all you can control." I believe that this is fruitful advice for the preaching ministry as well. There are a lot of things if we want to admit it or not that are not within our control, they are in the control of an all wise God. However, there are things that we do have within our control such as the way we use our time. We can control our perspective of how we read the biblical text and how we will use that perspective to assist people on their faith journey.

There are times that I believe intentionally or unintentionally the minister can duck or dodge the responsibility that has been divinely disseminated to them. Ministry certainly has an element of stewardship that is attached to these transcendent transactions. Talents and gifts exist in the minister in order to effectuate change and this will take initiative, it will take innovation, it will take courage, and it will take a drive and determination to see the assignment through which God has celestially crafted for your hands.

The interrogative question hovering over the preacher is, Can God count on you? There are those who are bent on passing the blame onto the church as a whole. There are those preachers that blame the conditions in which they are ministering. There are those that kneeled to nihilistic thoughts concerning the future of the church and the involvement of the people that are supposed to be committed to the church but are behaving as audible Christians and active atheist. There is a litter in language and linguistics that can tragically break the link of communication between the creation and the Creator which could be caused by the conduct of clergy. There are seekers that are pleading and looking for a shift in the direction of their lives, but if we only concentrate on the trouble and never look on the other side of the minted coin of grace, I believe as Paul Scott Wilson said, "We'll never see Christ in the crisis."

Chapter 5

No Matter What

There is an established tension that exist between the lettered preacher and the unlettered preacher; the preacher that is formally trained and the preacher that is informally trained; the preachers that are educated and the preachers that have not received institutional academic training. I believe that I am equipped to speak on this matter with conviction because I have benefited from both sectors. On the one hand being advised on the stump (as the southern preacher calls their counseling quarters) and on the other hand studying in the halls of academia. Frankly I believe there is an extreme need for both experiences because it exposes the preacher to a well-rounded view of ministry while battling against some avoidable biases.

The cemetery or the seminary

Too often I hear derogatory comments that are spewed from the pulpit degrading those who felt led to further educate themselves through formal seminary training. One statement that is prevalently made is: "All because you have degrees it doesn't mean you have the anointing." Concurrently, I have heard a couple of seminary trained preachers state: "If you don't have any degrees then you aren't eligible to preach for me." Clergy are accused of not taking their calling serious. Both of these views drip with a touch of a divisive dogmatic disposition towards an experience in ministry that they may be totally oblivious.

As I stated earlier, I am a preacher that has been blessed to experience the ecclesiastical preaching atmosphere as well as the sacred halls of academia that is proudly bent toward pedagogy. Residing in the church and seminary are benefits that are extraordinary. Both arenas must be sensitive and respectful concerning the complementary aspect of each. The role of the homiletic practitioner and the homiletic theorist are necessary pillars in the development of preachers and churches. The homiletic theorist inculcates a sobering message that at times may be upsetting to the equilibrium of the preacher which echoes from the throne of academia. They believe this contribution is necessary for the pulpiteer and or practitioner to reinforce the honoring of scholarly contributions. While those scholarly sound bites of the homiletic theorist are transferred through the cleric's canals, there are those who take seriously the garment of the *Witness of Preaching*. In the words of Thomas Long, "Challenging the theorists' implications of a flawless plan of homiletic remedies will affect change in the people."

The practitioner becomes a constant wakeup call or a chiming reminder that theory won't always neatly fit in the ecclesiastical sector because of the variables that are present in ministry. This causes preachers to consider that the theological waters could become quite murky as clergy navigate ministry across cultures and become more apprised of the dubious lines of denominational affiliations. Not to mention ministering to the para religious groups. These are the matters that must be considered as preachers attempt to preach in an ever-changing world.

In this Chapter, it is my desire to place emphasis on the importance of each side of the homiletic coin so to speak. Hopefully and effectively oscillating between formal and informal educational models of preaching. This will allow us to consider the vital role each offers in an ever-expanding partnership in the matter of preaching.

I have skills and I also have the Spirit

During my first couple of years in my preaching ministry, I was employed with the American Red Cross. At the time I was also attending Ashland Theological Seminary as a first-year seminarian to fulfill my God led calling to prepare myself for present and future ministry. On one occasion I had the opportunity to preach for a local pastor who worked for the company as well. The next day a fellow coworker who attended the worship service spoke very highly of the message but then came the cutting critique, "Wait until you start preaching with the Spirit you are really going to be special."

I was left speechless. First of all, it is humbling for anyone to refer to your preaching as great, but this is not what left me speechless. The part that caught me off guard was that she thought I was preaching without the Holy Spirit. The question that I had for this young lady was, "Are you saying that because I am using my God given intellect, I'm using a prepared vocabulary in order to articulate with precision and raising theological terms that may be foreign concepts to some of the congregants that you felt that the sermon was Spiritually bankrupt?"

Well, this young lady's observation concerning the lack of Connectivity of the Spirit in the message (no matter how absurd it may sound), this dogmatic charismatic thinking (if we could even call it that), is more prevalent in today's society and is found in many more places than we desire to admit. These individuals that believe brainless faith equals faithfulness is a travesty to the people that have to succumb to these vacant substantive(less) sermons. They believe the educated preacher has a self-reliance on him or herself. They continuously contest the preacher's focus on their own ability and strength. If these preachers use any of their training to assist in the transcendent transaction of sacred ministry their activity is viewed as out of line. These ministers that have an educational fervor to their teaching and preaching have been classified as Pharisees. The mere fact that these clergy seek knowledge and truth prior to the preaching moment doesn't mean that they detest or reject God's revelation of the word to them at the time of the preaching moment. This activity of insufficient interest in preparation is homiletically irresponsible and bears the marks of not having immunity to heresy.

There are several scriptural references used as an apologetic against those who use acumen instead of what they suggest is the real anointing: Acts 26:24 NASB *Much learning has made you mad*; Acts

4:13 NASB *They were ignorant and unlearned men and they marveled*; Luke 12:12 NASB *For at that time the Holy Spirit will teach you what you should say*. These are only a few scriptures among many used to demean the efforts of the preacher or minister whose desire is to prepare themselves for providing effective ministry.

I have had the privilege to travel as a dually aligned Professor of Homiletics and a National Preacher. I made a horrific discovery concerning the malnourished congregants of the body of Christ and this was across all denominational lines that I encountered. There are those who are more intrigued by catch phrases, slogans, syllogisms from the latest tweet or hashtag verbiage than being receptive to proper exegesis and a spiritual power packed presentation that is theologically color coded with investigation, application and explanation.

Exhilaration is found in expressions that are filled with erroneous theology and with insufficient promissory notes of delirious declarations that are not divinely appointed. Or, Sweaty Sideshows disguised as praise breaks of holy outburst that become exercises of oral gel excursions not returned once the sound of the music ceases.

God is an intellectual being. We serve a God that doctrinally we believe to be omniscient, the God who knows everything. There are certain reoccurring terms in the Bible which are based on the importance of those terms. One of the terms and principles that is repetitive in nature is the word **wisdom.** This virtue was vital to those who would be deemed as righteous. This virtue is so important that when we speak of Jesus Christ the son of God we call him the

Logos the *Word* because he is viewed as the living embodiment and the Transcript of the Wisdom of God. Jesus is God's wisdom in the flesh. This wisdom has an image of a garland which is perceived as a crown of wisdom or virtue. It is not strange then when Solomon was asked what he desired most, he asked for wisdom.

The usage of theology in the sermon should never be used to exalt one's self, but rather used to inspire men and women, boys and girls to experience their own face to face encounter with God because of the depths of the words retrieved from the preachers encounter with God themselves. Richard Lischer suggested in his text the *Theology of Preaching* that "Theology's exposition of the faith and its openness to the world corresponds with preaching's dual responsibility to the word and the world." (Lischer 2001, 5)

The sermon event should be an experience that is spirit filled and scholastically enlightening. John Nelson one of Wesley's laity preachers wrote of his first opportunity to hear Wesley preach: "It made my heart beat like the pendulum of a clock and as he spoke I thought his whole discourse was aimed at me. When he was done I said, this man can tell the secrets of my heart."

Theological Education Can Enhance the Preacher and Preaching

Theological Education's responsibility is not to call the preacher, its primary function is to prepare the preacher. Every week I have several calls from individuals concerning the desire to go to seminary or Bible College. One of the first questions that I ask is "Why do you desire to go and what is the end game for you?"

Surprisingly, one of the most neglected parts of selecting a seminary does not have to do with the theological courses which enhance your critical thinking, but the spiritual formational courses that challenge and check your perspective concerning your view of God, your view on the word of God and your view of the world. During my tenure in seminary, my professor, Dr. Wardle whom I owe a tremendous debt for my personal growth in the area of spiritual sensitivity introduced me to the writings of Henri Nouwen. One of the books that I read annually is *The Way of the Heart*. This text deals with spiritual heart issues that will ultimately influence the way in which you treat yourself and the people around you. It checks the motives of your heart. This is consciousness of the well-being of the heart is promoted in scripture. Jesus reminded us in the Matthean Gospel that "Where your treasure is that's where your heart will be also." He also on one occasion reprimanded the hypocrisy of the Pharisees by stating that "You cherish me with your lips, but your hearts are far from me." The herald must have a frequent heart checkup in ministry. Seminaries should offer this in the curriculum because ultimately, we serve people not a proclamatory practice.

The heart is very important because it is from the channel of the heart that real ministry flows. What will cause you to study? What will cause you to forgive those who offend you? What will cause you to have (ethos) integrity when you find yourself in situations that are not integrous? It's the spiritual formation not exclusively the knowledge of the formation of the text from a contextual and historical view.

The theological education process also enhances the preacher by challenging the embedded theologies that permeate in their pondering. My grandmother had a saying and that was "When you know better, then you should do better." Theological education exposes you to information such as authors, journals, seminars, and experiences that you will not encounter in the local church. There are concerns that need to be addressed concerning the Bible. But, for those who are unwilling to be open to reflection and questioning, they will never contribute one iota of thought into why a text is arranged in the way that it is or be aware that there are other extrabiblical sources that will assist in educating the people more deeply regarding their faith.

Theological education in homiletics has changed my world. I have discovered that there are various forms available to me concerning preaching. One of the epiphanies is the inductive versus the deductive preaching format. Fred Craddock's book *As One Without Authority* is a classic concerning the inductive methodology of preaching. There was a time when in seminary, there were questions of the relevancy of preaching courses in the seminary. Craddock injected that "The antibiotic of inductive preaching that caused a healing in the heads and hearts of those that were infected with a philosophy that the minister can divorce the dynamics of preaching from the preacher without causing a lifelong theological traumatic experience which would be existentially unbearable." And then there is the deductive method that I learned from Edward Branch while enrolled in my introductory course of preaching. In this course I was introduced to the *Certain Sound of a Trumpet*, written by Samuel Dewitt Proctor. It was in this book that I learned about the proposition. Proctor wrote this during a time when preachers really struggled with structuring their message, so that they would be organized and orally exciting. He instituted what Robert Smith Jr called in his text *Doctrine that Dances*. Proctor was informing those especially in the African American community, that you can have gravy and gospel without creating an exegetical gap and chasm that perpetuates the crisis of exegesis as Walter Kaiser refers to it in that marvelous text *Toward an Exegetical Theology of Preaching*.

Preachers can be exposed to valuable resources through theological education. These resources are designed to feed them and assist them in the fulfillment of perfecting the craft of preaching, all while finding models that will mold meanings that are saturated with antidotal accuracy and spiritual sacredness. I recall a format that I was introduced to in a seminar Proclaimers Place hosted by Joel Gregory. He spoke about many formats but one in particular was the diamond outline. This form allows you to turn the text and see the prism of the text; showing different facets that would have never been illumined if you didn't have a different look at the different characters or the different points of view of the metanarrative; or the format known as the bait and switch which goes like this: "is it this no! is it this no! is it that yes!" You intentionally give what it is not so that you can give emphasis to what it really is.

Being able to experience all of these possibilities and arrangements of formatting a sermon has as A. Louis Patterson states, "Open my mind theologically to the possibilities of what I can integrate in my homiletic in order that it can be theologically sturdy and communicated with *crystal clarity*." This is just a scanty amount of strategies and priceless take-aways that you can receive from theological education.

I Didn't go but I Did

In the African American tradition, there are so many that have been influenced by C.L. Franklin who is the biological father of the Queen of Soul, Aretha Franklin. This preacher was entrusted with the wind pipes of the angelic. When he preached there was a flawless cadence; a tamed but tantalizing talk; a richness of relevance that left those who listened to the sermon literally spell bound by his speaking. With all of the preachers that attempted to shape themselves or drew from his genius, the missing ingredient that is normally neglected was his home seminary courses.

Pastor C.L. Franklin had been taught in his home (according to those who knew Franklin personally) a seminary education. He received tutorial and classes in his home from a seminary instructor. Instead of him going to the seminary the seminary came to him. The point of this is that even though Franklin didn't go he did go to school. This is commendable because even with all of the gift that he possessed he felt the necessity to prioritize a place and space for him to receive training in order to become more effective in his preaching. This Mississippi preacher of course was in high demand. He traveled the length and breadth of the country but in his travels, he never left behind that old adage of the preacher and that is "get your learning and your burning!"

It came out of nowhere

There are those in ministry that when they began, they had no clue that they would rise so quickly in their preaching ministry. These preachers could not work and preach at the same time because the demand of their schedule was to arduous. Remember, this was during the era that if you were going to go to seminary or bible college or even the university, there were no long-distance learning models available. Online classes were not an option nor was there a reality for them. They had to go leaving behind sometimes what they knew for what they didn't know! The reason why some of those preachers did not attend seminary wasn't because they didn't believe in it, it was because they didn't have the necessary tools in that era which provided them with the ability to pull it off.

The Back-Porch Classroom

On numerous occasions, my Pastor Tellis Chapman shared with me nutritious nuggets concerning what the preachers in the south referred to as "the back porch or getting on the stump." He explained that this was during the time that the journeymen preacher would follow around the master of preaching (the season preacher) in order that they could learn the ropes of pastoring and how to preach effectively in different settings. Such as, preaching without notes; having a sermon in your head and your heart and that Wednesday is Thursday; Thursday is Friday; Saturday is a rest day and Sunday is a work day.

These are some of the concepts that a preacher could learn in an informal setting. Does this matter today? In a climate when after the preacher gets called yesterday then they feel like they are ready to pastor today? Does it matter in this ministerial climate where correction is a controversial communication viewed as treason to the aspiration of the new minister whose revelation of the scripture trumps your years of training and your experience as a pastor? Does it matter in a climate where the preacher feels that ordination means that they've been mysteriously overshadowed by the seed of pastoring and that a church is in them that needs birthing? All of this before the ink can even dry on the ordination license.

The informal theological hunches are just as important as formal theological education. During the time that you are learning informally, you will be provided with the working knowledge of the activity of the church and preaching. This occurs prior to your being introduced into homiletic theory. This allows you to get your feet wet so that you won't go into theological and/or homiletical shock when you first get to seminary. Paul Scott Wilson imparts to us "the way we all read scripture is held together and united in Christ" if we are trained or untrained ministers. (Wilson 2001, 58)

The first lesson of homiletics I received was at a desk in my pastor's office. I believe he saw my humility, my willingness to learn; my receptivity to correction and also my desire to get better and since that day, I have been on a pursuit for homiletic excellence. Each Sunday became an informal lesson. I would watch him preach and the consistency in which he preached. The passion, the drive, the excellence, the attention to detail, the obsessiveness over every little detail and, it fascinated me causing me to be somewhat of a nuisance, a pest for preaching. You can't become better if you are not a pest as a preacher. You must be tenacious about asking questions. After receiving the answers to those questions you have asked, you will find that you have begun to literally build, dig the foundation, pour the cement for stability, and put up the sermonic steal so that when the Professors come in they can create the structure around what is already an existing structure which has a firm foundation.

Unfortunately, there are preachers who think they have too much intellectual prowess to submit to the shaping of another preacher or they feel some kind of way about needing to be instructed and corrected as a preacher. From a biblical perspective this mindset is preposterous. Jesus was called Rabbi or Teacher. During those times in antiquity it was the disciple's responsibility to make sure that they were with their Rabbi at all times so that they could thoroughly learn the trade and tendencies of the teacher. The existing model of North America's educational system came from this model. I invite you to take the time to study the word *authority* in scripture. You will discover in the new testament, but particularly in the gospels, that the authority which the student possessed existed because it came from the Rabbi which they studied and had now in turn given them the authority and or the power.

What are the advantages of informal training

You create father son or mother daughter relationships. Paul in his writings, especially in Timothy, uses the word Teknon. This word literally means that Paul viewed Timothy like a blood son. Paul knew that Timothy's biological father was a Pagan and he needed fatherly spiritual guidance. When you have a pastor, a mentor, a coach this allows you to have a sermonic sound board to challenge your thinking, elevate your mind, and keep you morally accountable. There are things that you will receive that are invaluable so that when the tough and lonely days of ministry ahead arrive, you will hear the echoing of those words homiletically haunting you but in a good way telling you to *stay the course. It is not in word only and you cannot out preach a corrupt life.* These moments give you a certified core in ministry because you've canvassed enough clergy to now give a significant and sustaining contribution to ministry and this will allow future generations to receive beneficiary pay outs from your homiletic humility.

There is a need for Homiletic assimilationist. Those that can take what they have learned from both the informal setting and the formal theological setting and engrave substantial contributions in the hearts of people. Doing so could literally catapult them to a spiritual standard that is exquisite and a career path that breeds the inclusion of Christ.

Where would I be if I didn't humble myself and embrace the opportunity to carry the bag of the preacher(s)? It reminded me of when I would carry my bookbag to class. Where would I be if I failed to understand the priceless privilege it was to hang out like a wall flower in the office of the season preacher? Or, gathering the nuggets I'd over hear while hanging out at the library crafting exegetical papers? Where would I be if I didn't get the chance to ask questions of the seasoned preacher I was caring for? I cannot put enough emphasis on the tremendous value that can be found in asking the right questions from the right seasoned preacher; "What advice do you have for a younger preacher? That coupled with asking my professors questions such as, "What is the Telos of the Sermon? The blend; the mixture; the meshing together; the combination; the intermingling of these two institutions? In doing so, I have been granted breathtaking benefits from others who've travelled this road before, thus allowing me to benefit from their past experiences. John Witherspoon, in his lectures on moral philosophy, eloquence, and divinity, said that the best form of training is a wise study and imitation of great models. Arthur Hoyt, in The Work of Preaching, recommended that the preacher select one or two men who in some way especially spoke to him. (Wiersbe & Perry 1984, ix).

Several years ago, Rodney King, a black man who we have come to know of because of a recording of him being severely beaten by several white police officers during the Los Angeles riots asked a critical question, "Can we all just get along? We can engage in argumentation which is a formal discussion instead of arguing which leads to screaming and shouting beckoning to be right opposed to making people righteous. It is vital that we lay down our homiletic sermonic spears and shooters and preach this gospel like the men and women God has called us to be!

Chapter 6

What Matters the Most

Being cautious in ministry is beneficial but there is also a downside to that as well when we play it too safe and fail to step out on faith. The caution that I am delineating is indifference to your length of time in ministry. We as clergy must be sober minded, as well as careful to focus our attention on those things in the preaching ministry that will immensely impact our society and promote spiritual growth. I thought that it would be beneficial to draft a list of meditative and methodological practices in preaching which allows the preacher to maximize a predetermined aim; and display oratorical excellence and an enhancement of the sociological environments.

Clarity in Communication

One preacher suggested that you cannot be clever and expose the clarity of Christ at the same time. When there is an inclination to be impressive this tends to impair those hearers from obtaining a reservoir of behavioral and spiritual improvement. The craft of effective preaching is most profitable when the preacher is invisible but visible. When people can hear the proclamation of the gospel and they are engulfed in the essence of the word, Christ is exalted on the throne of their hearts while dismantling their infatuation or obsession with the personality of the preacher.

Now, lest I am misunderstood, there is a need for a preacher to have a keen presence. This presence should be based on the ethos or integrity of the preacher. There should be an iridescence that illuminates from the preacher because of their faithful fellowship with God. A preacher should be seen preaching. We are not supposed to be clergy that speak behind the curtain liken unto the wizard on the *Wizard of Oz*. When we preach we should show up! How many times has the preacher shown up, nicely dressed, groomed, smothered with the finest cologne and exhibit class and style but once you take a closer look you find that there is nothing substantive! This is not just a physiological showing up, it is a communicative showing which means your sermon should never be a no show or a useless meaningless exercising of speech for the hearer. When you preach you should show up in person and in pronouncement.

What are some ways that we can avoid this problematic pronouncing? Have a game plan, an oratorical mapping of where you desire to take the listener. One thing I can suggest in this regard is to incorporate components of structure. This will not offer a guarantee but, it will increase the likelihood that the people that are listening to you will have a sense of what you are communicating in the sermon.

When the sermon has a Major Concern; Fallen Condition Focus; a Sermonic Claim; a Proposition, these will draw attention to the Main Focus of the passage and will eliminate what shouldn't be said. In addition, this will make your voice the most valuable principle that's evident in that particular sermonic event. Now this may differ from preacher to preacher because we are preaching with diverse personalities, but we can not select where we place the weight or what is emphasized in the passage.

There are those who build a hermeneutic but totally ignore the Telos of the passage. This is the under girding thematic thrust of what this writer deems important to share with the people. "Crossing the principled bridge" as Duvall says in *Grasping God's Word* is important. Honoring the original order of the passage in antiquity and transferring that into an oratorical delivery that helps people overcome their present obstacles is what matters in preaching today.

Collecting from other Contributors

The practice of preaching was not constructed on a Lone Ranger practicum. Those that attempt to preach the gospel with integrity and accuracy execute a prevalent search for other preachers which they can learn from (past and present). Church Father Augustine wrote in *On Christian Doctrine* that speaking is best learned by studying Christian speakers and that good style in preaching is more caught than taught, which is accomplished by exposure to the great speakers. (Wiersbe & Perry 1984, ix) When you look over the conglomerate of opportunities that we have to learn from, we find available a vast selection of books, recordings and experiences that are worth investing our time and that'll help in removing us out of homiletical entrenchment. Unfortunately, there are some that believe that homiletics is limited to two races of people, Caucasian and African American. Homiletics can't be reduced to the monopoly of only these two cultures when there are so many others. There are preachers that believe in Christ from different cultures whose voices are suppressed because they are dominated by the supposed two leading voices in America.

We would do well to discover the challenges in the Hispanic culture and who are their top homileticians. Or, how about India, who has requested that I come to give a series of homiletic lectures across a period of several days (translator provided)? This is a scanty list among so many others that communicate the gospel in marvelous ways that also encourage them to holistic living in Christ. The effectiveness of each culture's ability to share the gospel story and connect people with God has intrigued me in my Homiletics study. The question of what is the nuts and bolts that hold these different arguments and conversations (homily) together? Each of us can learn from each other realizing that it is profitable to grasp an understanding of how massive the gospel is across the globe.

On one occasion I received an early text from my Pastor (It is always my intention to not allow a week to go by without some sort of communication between us). He texted me these words: "I challenge you to take the time and reach back to the preachers of the past and it will set your soul on fire." Of course, anyone who knows me knows that I am always up for a challenge that'll aid me in my growth. I came across a jewel and that was Samuel Dewitt Proctor's sermon *When religion attempts to make it without Jesus.* Wow, what a title! This is the challenge I believe of today's preacher and that is that possibly pulpits are trying to make good without the one in whom they are commissioned to preach about. It is a sad day when there are those who leave the name of Jesus out of there sermons so that people don't get offended. Jesus Christ causes a direct challenge for the preacher to be conformed to Him and not to conform to the activity of the popular culture. We need a reminder forever theologically buzzing in our creative homiletic ear to remain theologically strong and ecclesiastically sensitive to the moving of the pillar of the church culture liken unto the pillar in Exodus.

If I may pose a challenge of my own, try to find preachers out of your normal listening rotation. Take time out and search for female theologians in homiletics one of which I would highly recommend is Dr. Teresa Fry Brown. Search for other preachers that are separate from the dominant culture that I just mentioned. If you are not a seminary student read a seminary professors sermon or listen to their preaching. I encourage you to take time and examine the pattern of pondering of Christ through the lens of a Catholic theologian like Raymond E Brown. If you are a seminary trained preacher search for preaching traditions that are not familiar. In doing this exercise, you must be intentional in your efforts to disarm your embedded preferences so that you don't default your hearing to what you are accustom to. You must engage in intentional listening.

The different levels of expertise in homiletics grants us multiple ways that can deepen our understanding of what is at the core of preaching. If you relieve us of our props in 'preacherdom' how effective would we really be. The challenge that we face isn't if we can be effective in the culture in which we are accustom to (a culture that to a certain extent, already agrees to the message and the delivery system as well) but, when we are nudged toward those methods that are beyond our norms. We must the question of ourselves: "Can I effectively take the contributions of others and give a solid message that is compassionate but without compromise?"

During my Tenth Pastoral Anniversary banquet, Dr. Marvin McMickle stated to me that "If you see a turtle on a fence to remember one thing is for sure, it didn't get there by itself." Someone had to lift it up to that height. Bill Hybels in his book *Simplify* further impressed upon us that, "None of us got where we are in life today 100 percent on our own power" (Hybels 2013,64). It was because of invaluable contributions that were freely given to us by others who were concerned and considerate enough to share their spiritual blessings with us in order that we may weigh in on a better understanding, finding a finer way to articulate the oracles of God. We should not take undue credit for this impartation but, continue the flow of homiletic insight and impressions on others, encouraging them to receive the gospel with homiletic honesty.

Center of Emotion

When I articulate my own personal perspective of preaching I classify it as heart preaching. If there is any success in my preaching whatsoever it comes from the involvement of my heart as a part of my utility. I believe preaching should come from a pure place of love, compassion, sincerity, and a true concern for the people. The cardia in scripture is not speaking of the heart that is in your chest which has veins and vessels and a heartbeat that promotes blood flow. The cardia most of the time in scripture is speaking about the seat of the emotions which is the mind.

The center of emotions is the mind which is ultimately connected with your heart. I believe that there needs to be a healthy balance between the two. I believe that it's not a good idea for us to minister out of pure emotions because we can unknowingly detour from theological truth. The goal is not to make people feel better in a circumstance that is not getting better but worst. Our goal is to empower them to confront it. On the other hand, there is also a need for the preacher not to be too heady because this can come off as callous and cold to those who are seeking comfort. There are times that there may need to be graphed within the message a homiletic hug. These are words that arrest you and melt the massive stone that has been erected in one's heart but, with enough godly guidance through the scriptures they can receive spell binding comfort.

Cost of Ministry

Most don't put much effort into that which cost them little or nothing. Not often do people mention how much Jesus's disciples had to give up to seriously heed to Jesus call in the early parts of Luke, "follow me." Peter had to give up his thriving business of fishing which likely yielded great profit; Matthew was a tax collector; James the Zealot had to leave from insurrection; James and John forsook their father. There is a cost to ministry that you have to endure if you are to fulfill the demanding call of that ministry.

During a conversation with a younger preacher, I was asked the question, "How do you become a great preacher." My response to him was a question, "Are you willing to allow portions of your life to literally pass you by? The barbecues; the invites to various events; the nice cool spring days when people are having picnics (gnat and mosquito free) *Lol*; taking a stroll on a summer day enjoying an ice cream cone or how about the lost sleep, rising early at 4:00am in order that you may have your intimacy with God so you never lose sight of why you do what you are doing in the first place. There is a cost for ministry and there are not too many that are willing to agree to the terms and conditions or the privacy policy of ministry. They ultimately walk away as a form of disagreeing to do it.

Now let us be clear, I did not state that your obligation to ministry gives you permission to have terrible stewardship over your family life and your church. Ministers are not supposed to be Intra Incurvatus in se (that is interest curved in on self). We are not in ministry so that we can maximize our own personal gains while others are dehydrated in their attempt to keep up with our pace. We must be mindful that there are those who are caring for their families and fulfilling their God commissioned responsibility, but we are guilty of neglecting our families and wondering why they cannot keep up. You are gaining more hours in the day based on what you do not face opposed to becoming the example to those that you are supposed to be feeding and helping to grow in faith.

The way that we can find true value in a ministry that Matters today is by leading people to their divine destiny. This is when preaching truly matters: To hear stories about suicidal individuals that have found their purpose for living and now are walking down a path of wholeness and awareness of the abiding power and love of God reminds us that preaching matters; preaching matters when we see that young lady or young man being pressured to engage in ill-fated activities. Instead they choose to remain steadfast in their beliefs and ignore the intimidation tactics. They then go on to make the choices that lead to transformation consequently impacting a school, a club, etc. Preaching Matters when the college student gets impregnated and believes that her life is over, she is also under the misconception that Christ forgiveness is not powerful enough to get her through her circumstance but, the gospel wills her back to spiritual health, accountability and responsibility that allows her to raise her child while regaining her focus and making no excuses in her attempt to get the required grades. Preaching Matters to those that have had some major false starts in their lives. They believe that their mistakes define them and there is no realistic way out of the circumstances that continue to plague their lives. But, they discover a relentless hope that has hope inside of hope that propels them forward.

You may ask the question, What Matters? My response is:

Preaching that is Authentic

Preaching that is Transformative

Preaching that is Inspiring

Preaching that is Instructional

Preaching that is Convicting

Preaching that is Others Centered

Preaching that is Christ Centered

Preaching that is Filled with Hope

Preaching that is Comforting

Preaching that is Challenging

Preaching that is Selfless

Preaching that is Biblical

Preaching that is not Exclusive but Inclusive

Preaching that is Passionate

Preaching that Transcends Culture

Preaching that is Socially Conscious

Preaching that Makes a Difference

Preaching is Life Giving... Does Preaching Matters??? I believe this list is only a tip of the iceberg as to what preaching really means to our past, our present and our future. No matter who you are, if you have been called to preach let me inform you that preaching is infused with extraordinary abilities. The gift of preaching has been entrusted to us by God to lead, guide and direct you through life whether it be on the interstate or on the streaming networks of the future. It is my belief that preaching will never be dethroned as the primary form of proclamation that will position the world for the Parousia of Christ.

Preach Passionately my Friends
Dr. Chat!
#GoBeGreat

Biography

Dr. Aaron L. Chapman, a servant of God, is often referred to as a relevant power packed Minister of the priceless Gospel of our Lord and Savior Jesus Christ.

An alumnus of Murray Wright High School, Rev. Chapman graduated in the top five percent (3%) of his class. He was accepted to Eastern Michigan University, and shortly thereafter his academic achievement was further honored by being placed on the Dean's list. In December 2003, he received a Bachelor of Science Degree in Communications with a Minor in General Business from Eastern. In January 2004, he began his pursuit for a Dual Master's Degree in Divinity and Theology at Ashland Theological Seminary. In June

2006, Rev. Chapman graduated with honors from Ashland with a Masters of Divinity Degree. In his desire to be all that God had called him to be, Dr. Aaron L. Chapman in 2011 received an earned Doctoral Degree from Ashland Theological Seminary.

At present, Dr. Chapman serves as a professor in Homiletics at Ashland Seminary and a professor at the Heritage Center in Denominational Studies and several other educational institutions including: Ecumenical Seminary, Grace College, Moody theological Seminary, Manthano College, Triumph Church Institute, Michigan North Central Ecclesiastical Jurisdiction (Bishop Sheard presiding) and his very own Seminary on Wheels in Southfield MI. He is also the Author of the newly released books "Preaching without Heart", "I'm Called to Preach now What?" and Leaving Life's Envelope Empty and Mining for Masterpieces.

Dr. Aaron L. Chapman served as a faithful member of Galilee Missionary Baptist Church for eleven (11) years where he was called to preach the gospel under the tutelage of Rev. Dr. Tellis J. Chapman. On April 23, 2005. God called him to Pastor the Dedicated To Christ Baptist Church. Dedicated To Christ held their first worship service on September 4, 2005, at 19400 Evergreen in Detroit, Michigan in the St. Timothy Lutheran Church. Through the grace of the Lord and Leadership of Dr. Aaron L. Chapman, Dedicated To Christ purchased their new church home at 4424 8th Street in Ecorse Michigan in October, 2007.

Within the ranks of the local, State, and National Conventions and Congresses, Dr. Chapman is the newly appointed Homiletics Professor of the National Baptist Convention USA INC. Homiletics Instructor for BM&E State Convention, Vice President of DIMA, Former Congress President for the Central District Association, and sought after Homiletics conference speaker. He has received Christian Education certificates in the Holy Spirit Doctrine; Building Effective Ministries and Pastors Seminars.

Since the inception of Dedicated to Christ, Dr. Chapman has established several ministries: Drama Ministry, Evangelism, Media, Music/Praise Ministry, Nurses, Operation Bread Basket, Operation "Big Give", Recreation, Security, Shepherds Care, Dedicated To Christ Bookstore, DTC Café, Men, Women and Youth Ministries, Dance Ministry, Stick Squad, Audio/Visual Ministry, Godly Guidance Ushers Ministry, My Bridges (DHS), Heavenly Hands Up Food Pantry, Dedicated to Christ Website, Dedicated to Christ phone app and Destine For Greatness Childcare. For five (5) years he has served as founder and leader of Dedicated to Christ's Biblical Impartation Class.

Dr. Aaron Chapman is married to the former Valarie Kay Wilkinson and they are the proud parents of two children Aaron Christian and Destiny Kay Chapman.

References

Allen, O Wesley. 2008 *Determining the Form*. Minneapolis: Fortress Press.

Bovon, Francois 2019. *Hermeneia*, Luke1. Minneapolis Fortress Press.

Brown-Taylor, Barbara. 1993. *The Preaching Life*. United Kingdom: Rowman & Littlefield.

Chapell, Bryan. 2005. *Christ-Centered Preaching*. Grand Rapids: Baker Academic.

Craddock, Fred. 1985. *Preaching*. Nashville: Abingdon Press.

Crocker, Lionel. 1971. *Harry Emerson Fosdick & Art of Preaching*. Illinois: Charles C Thomas Publisher.

Duduit, Michael. 1992. *Handbook of contemporary Preaching*. Nashville: Broadman Press.

Ells, Afred, and Gary Kinnamen. 2003. *Leaders that Last*. Grand Rapids, MI: Bakers Books.

Hybels, Bill. 2014. *Simplify*. Illinois: Tyndale House Publishers

Liske, Thomas.1960. *Effective Preaching*. New York: The Macmillian Company.

Long, Thomas. 2005. *The Witness of preaching 2nd Ed.* Louisville Kentucky: Westminster John Knox Press.

Maxwell, John. 2012. *The 15 invaluable Laws of Growth.* New York: Center Street Publisher.

McClure, John. 2007. Preaching Words. Louisville Kentucky: Westminster John Knox Press.

McMickle, Marvin. 2018. *The Making of a Preacher.* Valley Forge PA: Judson Press.

Packer, J.I.. 1986. *The Preacher and Preaching.* Phillipsburg New Jersey: P&R Publishing.

Perry, Lloyd and Wiersbe, Warren. 1984. *The Wycliffe Handbook of Preaching &Preachers.* Chicago: Moody Press.

Proctor, Samuel. 1994. *The Certain Sound of the Trumpet.* Valley Forge PA: Judson Press.

Smith, Robert. 2008. *Doctrine That Dances.* Nashville: B&H Publishing Group.

Stewart, James. 1946. *Heralds of God.* London. Hodder & Stoughton.

Wilson, Paul. 2001. *God Sense.* Nashville: Abingdon Press.